DREAM GUIDE

An Unofficial Guide to Walt Disney World for 2022 - 2024

by Adam Hattan

The *Hattan* Company

The Hattan Company

Unit 9 Overfield
Thorpe Way
Banbury
OX16 4XR
United Kingdom

ISBN: 978-1-9160897-7-8

For information about custom editions, special sales, premium or corporate purchases, please contact The Hattan Company Ltd. at contact@adamhattan.com

DREAM GUIDE

An Unofficial Guide to Walt Disney World for 2022 - 2024

by Adam Hattan

Whilst every effort has been made to ensure the content of this book is accurate, over time this information will become out of date. For this reason, please consult with your travel agent or with Walt Disney World directly for updated information on shows, attractions, dining locations, merchandise, offers, prices etc.

The publisher cannot accept responsibility for changes, errors or omissions in information provided within this book or for the consequences of any reliance by users on the information provided within this book.

Reviews and advice on particular elements of a visit to Walt Disney World including but not limited to attractions, shows, dining locations and resort hotels are those based on the authors own experience and opinion. Your experience may differ from those described within this guide.

You're welcome to write to the publisher to share your feedback on this issue or ideas/suggestions for future issues.

The Hattan Company Ltd.
Unit 9 Overfield
Thorpe Way
Banbury
OX16 4XR
United Kingdom

CONTENTS

INTRODUCTION

For millions of people around the globe, Disney offers an escape from the real world. Whether it's for the length of a movie, song, television show or theme park attraction, Disney has the special ability to help us dream a little bit more than we're used to. Walt Disney World is a destination to escape the real world and live amongst your wildest dreams. With state-of-the-art attractions, world class entertainment, exceptional dining and more, it's the number one tourist destination in the world for a reason.

The pandemic was a trying time for all of us. Now, we get to wish upon a star again and look forward to a holiday that doesn't have a better chance of being cancelled, than it does actually going ahead. Whilst a lot has changed since the pandemic, a Walt Disney World holiday is still truly magical and unlike anything else. Whilst you may need to loosen your purse strings and pack your patience for some of the changes, I'm here to guide you through the whole process and ensure you still have the best holiday possible (whilst keeping your budget in mind).

Having previously worked in Walt Disney World for two years, holidayed there in my teens and now regularly visiting the resort as part of my job, I've got a few tips and tricks that'll help you get the most out of your holiday. Rest assured, I've done the leg work for you and carefully curating what I know with what I love, to impart some useful information to help you plan, book and enjoy your trip.

Whilst there's a lot to learn and maybe some compromises to be made, you and I are going to cover everything you need to know before your dream Disney holiday. Not only that, I'll do my best to help you save your pennies and use your time wisely.

I've designed this guide in a way that is a little more tailored than other guides out there. I'll recommend hotels, dining and attractions based on what you actually like and want! Additionally, I'll hand you some extra-special tips, tricks and lesser known facts of the resort, to make this more than just your average guidebook.

Walt Disney World is where I've had the pleasure of growing up, it's where I discovered my passions in life and lived out my wildest dreams. Disney means the world to me and Walt Disney World is somewhere I really consider a home away from home. I honestly want you to experience the best of what this magical place has to offer and have a trip that will provide you with everlasting happy memories.

Whether you're planning your 1st or 51st visit, it's my wish that this guide will hold your hand and show you everything you didn't know you needed to know. Kick back and relax, I'm here to bring the magic directly to you and ensure your next trip to Walt Disney World is as magical as can be.

- Adam Hattan

Chapter 1
HOW TO USE DREAM GUIDE

Dream Guide is here to advise you and your family, specifically based on your demographic, likes, dislikes and priorities. Each section of Dream Guide is divided up into the different stages of planning and enjoying your Walt Disney World holiday.

Within each section, I've provided information tailored to all manor of family units. So whether you're a singleton, couple or family of 10 or more, you'll be able to find the tips and tricks that will make your holiday special. To make Dream Guide as simple as can be, I'll be using some rating systems and handy icons to help you find what's right for you quickly and easily.

It's Written in the Stars

Throughout Dream Guide, you'll find these star ratings. These will help me communicate my priority rating for each element I'm discussing. Sometimes they'll be related to a specific subject (e.g. a hotel's location) or they'll show you whether a particular attraction is a must-do or a 'if we have time' kinda thing.

One Star

Don't think for one moment that one star means it's terrible. It just means that based on my experience, your time may be better spent elsewhere.

Two Stars

At a two star rating, I don't want to discourage you from trying it as it may be right for you. In my experience however, it's not on my list of priorities.

Three Stars

Three stars indicates that it's worth your time. See if you can make time for this but if you miss it, it's something you can do next time.

Four Stars

You'll want to make time for this. Having experienced most of what Walt Disney World has to offer, this is one of my favourites.

Five Stars

An absolute must-not-miss or one of my best recommendations for your trip! I don't hand out five stars for just anything.

One Size Does Not Fit All

You and your family are all individuals. You all have your own interests, likes and dislikes. However, when it comes to family units, space and suitability is one thing we can all agree is important on a holiday. For that reason, the below family unit icons will help you navigate what is likely suitable for you.

Single Adult

Having travelled on my own to Disney on a number of occasions, these are my recommendations if you're flying solo.

Adult Couple / Adult Friendship

Whether you're having a romantic getaway or going away with a friend, these will offer some great magic for both of you.

Honeymoon Couple

Whether on your actual honeymoon or a dedicated romantic retreat, these recommendations will have a little more sparkle.

Adults with Children

No matter how old your little ones are, these recommendations will give you some high quality family time.

Large Family

If you're taking the parents, the kids, the grandparents and the kitchen sink, these suggestions should work for everyone.

Grandparents / Experienced Adults

If you're bringing your parents/grandparents or you're an 'experienced adult,' these options may suit a steadier pace.

Single Parent

Regardless of age, if you're taking your little one away by yourself, these recommendations should be right for you.

Attraction Icons

On-Ride Photo

Choose these attractions if you're looking to put Disney Photopass to good use (page 104).

Lightning Lane

This icon refers to attractions that have the option to skip the main line with Lightning Lane access. (page 81).

Money, Money, Money

A trip to Walt Disney World is not cheap, there's no secret about that. There are however ways to visit Disney without breaking the bank. If you're willing to be mindful about your spending before and during your holiday, you can avoid coming home with a crazy high credit card bill. Use the below icons to be mindful of how certain activities may effect your holiday spending.

Lower Cost

If you make an effort to use these options throughout your trip, you're less likely to have a heart attack when you see how much you've spent. Using dining as an example, these meals should cost $30 or less, per adult.

Average Cost

These options will be pretty common within the guide. They'll be the typically affordable destinations within your holiday. Using the same dining example as above, you'll be looking at approximately $50 per adult.

Higher Cost

Higher cost options are tailored for those not looking to hold back and those looking for a special treat within their holiday. Using the dining example, expect to spend anything upwards of $80 per adult.

Weather

Florida is one of the most unpredictable climates in the world. Within just a few minutes it can go from gorgeous sunny weather to something out of a disaster movie. The weather can be difficult to navigate when you're trying to stick to a plan or you're just not sure what you're looking for. These icons will help you decide on attractions and dining locations that will suit the current weather.

Sunny & Warm

Consider this as your 'all systems go' indicator. If this is next to something, it's my recommendation that this location is best enjoyed with warm or clear weather.

Hot & Humid

Florida can get dangerously hot. It's with this, you'll find recommendations that give you a chance to get out of the heat and cool down a little.

Thunder Storms

Thunder storms may be cool but they're incredibly dangerous and arrive regularly in the Orlando area. If you see this symbol, you'll know it's a good option, even in very worst weather.

Rain

If it's not a thunder storm you're in for, expect to at least see some rain. These recommendations will help you dodge and prepare for wet weather during your stay.

Chapter 2
ACCOMMODATION

Walt Disney World really is a world! With over 25 on-site resort hotels, in all manor of price brackets, it's easy to get a little overwhelmed by choice. Plus with options for off-site, villas and more, it's hard to know where to start.

Let's start off by walking you through the on-site options. These hotels are located on Disney property and offer some benefits and amenities that might be right for you. Then we'll look at some alternatives in case an off-site hotel or villa, may be better for you and your family (not to mention your budget).

Disney Resort Hotels (On-Site)

Disney categorises their hotels into three main tiers: Value, Moderate and Deluxe. First we'll take a look at the benefits of an on-site hotel and then dive into the tiers to find you some great options. Whilst prices vary based on time of year and availability, maybe choose a hotel in each category and go from there.

MagicBands

These seemingly simple bands have a whole lot of magic inside them! Using a MagicBand offers a whole lot of convenience. Let's take a look at everything this band can do if you're staying in a Disney hotel:

Change: MagicBands are no longer free as part of a Disney resort stay. They can now be purchased at most merchandise stores, starting at about $20.00 each.

- Your hotel room door magically opens with just a tap of your MagicBand.
- Your MagicBand can be linked to your room charging abilities. This saves you having to carry your wallet and gives you the freedom to pay for meals, merchandise and snacks whilst out and about. Don't worry, you have to enter a unique pin for each purchase, so there's security in place to make sure no one else can use your MagicBand if you loose it.
- Your MagicBand links to your My Disney Experience account (page 75), allowing you to use purchased Lightning Lane access, to download your Photopass photos and use your tickets to enter the parks.
- If you choose to purchase a Disney Dining Plan, this information is also linked to your band. So when dining, all you'll need to do is scan your MagicBand and sign the receipt. At a quick service location, it's just a tap.

Key to the World Card

If you'd rather not purchase a MagicBand, you'll be given a plastic card known as your Key to the World card.

This will do everything listed above and works just like a MagicBand. It'll act as your room key, park ticket, allow you to charge to the room etc.

The only downside with a card over a MagicBand, is having to take it out and put it away every time you use it. In my experience, a MagicBand is worth it.

PRO TIP

Whilst you can link MagicBands to your My Disney Experience account with the serial number on the back, the front desk can do it in mere seconds.

Complimentary Transportation

Disney is equipped to get you anywhere on property, free of charge. Disney's bus, boat, monorail and Skyliner services get you as close to the main entrance as you can get. For the most part, it's reliable, has regular service and is very convenient.

Stay in the Magic

An added benefit of staying in Disney, is you're always wrapped in Disney's outstanding guest service and exceptional theming. No matter where you are on your holiday, Disney will be taking care of you the whole time.

You're also close to all the fun! If you've been to Disneyland Paris or Disneyland Resort in California, you might be thinking 'oh we'll just save our money and stay near-by.' Slight problem with that however, no other resort is 'close' to the Disney parks in Florida. Disney owns some 30,000 acres, which means only Disney resorts are within a 15 minute journey of the attractions. Some hotels are even close enough to walk to one of the theme parks or Disney Springs.

Extra Time in the Theme Parks for Disney Hotel Guests

By staying in a Disney resort hotel, you get to benefit from some extra time in the theme parks. This time may give you the chance to get in line for some of the most popular attractions ahead of regular day guests or stay in the parks late.

Early Entry: If you're staying in a Disney resort, you'll be allowed to enter the theme parks ahead of the official opening time. Whilst this is traditionally 30 minutes prior to opening, Disney has been known to extend this time during peak seasons. To access Early Entry, all you have to do is scan through the ticket turnstiles (or tapstiles as they're known at Disney) and follow the signage to have your MagicBand or Key to the World Card scanned by a cast member. Regular day guests will be held back from this point until the official opening time comes and they're allowed to proceed to attractions.

Extended Evening Hours: If you're staying in a deluxe Disney resort hotel, Disney Vacation Club resort or select partner hotel, you'll be able to spend an extra two hours or so in select theme parks after regular closing time. Whilst Early Entry is every day at every park, Extended Evening Hours are only available one or two nights per week. Times will be advertised on the opening hours calendar on Walt Disney World's website.

To use these hours, you'll just need to present your MagicBand or Key to the World Card when entering the lines for attractions after regular park closing.

Change: The above benefits have replaced the formerly known and now discontinued Extra Magic Hours.

PRO TIP

To get the most out of your time in the parks, avoid joining lines for popular attractions at/around park opening. Since most guests will make a B-line for these rides, this is when the lines tend to be longest.

How to Choose a Disney Resort

Choosing a hotel can sound like a daunting task. Fear not, as I'll walk you through the different price tiers, give you my honest opinions of each hotel and share whether I think they're right for you or not.

Try creating a shortlist of three or four resorts as you go through. This will give you some flexibility when you start looking at availability and price. There's nothing worse than setting your heart on one resort, only to find out it's fully booked.

Whilst reading through the price tiers, be mindful of the following tips:

★ Whilst a value resort should in theory be cheaper than a moderate resort, there are some exceptions to the rule. I'll explain when we come to booking later on, but always compare a couple of hotels and room types, I wouldn't ever just pick and book.
★ Getting carried away at this stage could ruin your holiday. It's exciting choosing your hotel but know your budget and stick to it. Spending too much on a room that you're not using all day every day, may take precious coins away from other experiences.
★ Know how and where to book. I'll show you how to book your Disney holiday in the best way to ensure you get the best price (page 89).

What's actually at a Disney resort?

Sure, Disney resorts have some benefits attached to them but what's really there? You may be spending a number of weeks at this resort after all. Here's a breakdown of what's featured at all Disney resorts; regardless of price tier.

⭐ **Swimming Pool**: Most Disney resorts feature a themed pool and a 'quiet' pool. Around the main pool during the day, the kids activity cast members will be there to entertain your little ones and these pools are lifeguarded. Quiet pools don't tend to 'close.' As long as you're respectful of the rooms nearby, you could quite happily enjoy a late night swim. However, these pools aren't often lifeguarded, so it's best to supervise kids.

⭐ **Arcade**: Sometimes the only thing that will keep the little ones quiet for 30 minutes is arcade games. Just load up a game card and let the kids (and big kids) play until their heart's content (or until they run out of points and come bargaining for more).

⭐ **Laundry Facilities**: As much as we all try to avoid it, you may need to wash some clothes whilst you're away. Each resort features washer and dryer facilities, as well as vending machines with detergent and dryer sheets for purchase. These only accept credit/debit cards however.

* **Quick Service Dining**: Quick service refers to fast food. Whilst your mind may jump straight to burgers and chicken nuggets (which they do serve), you may also find 'make your own pasta' bars, sandwich stations, bakeries and special selections tailored to the resort theming. e.g. Mexican specialties at Disney's Coronado Springs.

* **Parking**: If you choose to rent a car when you arrive at Orlando International Airport, parking is available at all on-site hotels. However, there are parking charges to consider. For value resorts this is $15 a night. The price increases to $20 a night at moderate resorts and $25 a night at deluxe resorts.

* **Bus Station**: No matter which resort you choose to stay at, they all feature a bus station to take you to the parks, Disney Springs and the water parks (sometimes an in-direct service).

* **Merchandise**: Disney will always make sure you've got plenty of opportunity to purchase your souvenirs. Some resort shops are even better than in the parks!

* **Bar**: Don't worry parents, there's alcohol not too far away if it all gets a bit much. Whilst these may be a basic pool bar, most bars offer a varied menu and excellent service.

PRO TIP

The drinking age in the state of Florida is 21 years old. Cast members are required to request ID of anyone they think may be around or under 30 years of age. Have valid ID on you! UK travellers, be sure to read page 103.

Value Resorts

Value resorts tend to offer you the best of both worlds if you're used to staying off Disney property. They won't wring you dry of every penny but they will open the door to some of the on-site magic.

Of course, these resorts aren't the best of what's on offer at Disney but you'll likely find these hotels go above and beyond what's available off-site. Both in theming and amenities.

The majority of value resorts have also recently undergone refurbishment. Now, standard two queen rooms, have one of the beds as a pull-down, which doubles as a small dining table. These offer a little more space when you need it.

Benefits of Value Hotels

★ Cheapest resorts for a standard two queen bed room.
★ Ample number of rooms so it's often easier to book a stay (if doing so in advance).
★ Hugely family-friendly. With their quirky theming and huge pools, the kids will love a value resort.
★ Affordable family suites are available at value hotels, so you can be together whilst also enjoying plenty of space.

What Disney Won't Tell You

★ At certain times of day, buses will service multiple resorts. This means bus rides may take longer and it may be difficult to get a seat.
★ The rooms cover what you need but not always what you want.
★ These hotels will often host tour groups and larger group bookings. As such, the rooms are often more used than others and there may be some noise disruption.
★ The theming can look a little 'vegas.'

1. Disney's Art of Animation Resort

Featuring family suite room combinations in Finding Nemo, Lion King and Cars themes, this is a great place to stay with a family of 4 or more. Because of the room combinations, this resort will often be more expensive than other values. However, for 4-6 guests, suites are often cheaper than booking two rooms.

Linked with Pop Century (below) the resort offers a Skyliner service to Epcot and Hollywood studios. There are also a collection of Little Mermaid themed standard rooms which are similar in price to other standard rooms at the other value resorts. Just note, these are due for a refurbishment. All-in-all, it's a fun value resort with good offerings for the price.

BEST FOR	VALUE FOR MONEY	LOCATION

2. Disney's Pop Century Resort

ADAM'S CHOICE - If you're looking for the value resort that offers you the most for your money, look no further than Pop Century. The resort is themed with oversized icons from the 60's through to the 90's and is great for nostalgia! This resort also benefits from not being too big. No matter where your room is, it won't take you long to get to the bus station, Skyliner or quick service.

I love this resort for when it's just myself or when I'm with a friend. The only downside is that as it's a fan favourite, availability is very patchy. You may want to consider booking this one as far in advance as you can. If you get the chance to visit, even whilst staying elsewhere, be sure to get the chocolate chip pancakes! Honestly, one of the best value quick-service breakfasts on property.

BEST FOR	VALUE FOR MONEY	LOCATION
	 ✦ ✦ ✦ ✦ ✦	✦ ✦ ✦ ✦ ✦

PRO TIP

If you choose to stay at Art of Animation or Pop Century, keep in mind that lines for the Skyliner can get pretty long just before the theme parks open. The best way to avoid a long wait, is to travel at least an hour before park opening or at/just after park opening.

3. Disney's All Star Resorts

If you're looking for the cheapest stay possible, you'll likely find All Star Music, All Star Movies or All Star Sports to be your best option. These three hotels are basically one big hotel split into three different themes. Each separate theme has its own quick service, bus station, pool etc. Consider these resorts for a last minute trip, as you can often get an amazing deal staying here.

The All Star Resorts are favourites for large tour groups. If there's a cheerleader convention when you're planning on being in town, you may find a lack of availability or a higher rate per room. The bus routes will also sometimes service each resort as one. Making a 10 minute drive to Disney Springs a 45 minute bus journey on a pretty packed bus.

The savings are great here and you do still get the perks of being 'in Disney' but for me, if you're not planning on using the on-site perks to the max, you may find similar hotels for cheaper off property.

BEST FOR	VALUE FOR MONEY	LOCATION

Moderate Resorts

Moderate resorts are often the best bang for your buck. They offer more luxuries than value resorts but shouldn't cost you the earth and the world.

Whilst moderate resorts aren't as close to the parks as Deluxe resorts, they're certainly closer than the value resorts. They also sometimes offer extra transport options that may come in handy.

They also offer you that extra level of theming; going beyond something quirky to something atmospheric.

Benefits of Moderate Hotels

★ Best price for the amenities and comfort you can achieve from a Disney resort.

★ Multiple bus stops mean you're never too far away from a bus to the parks.

★ A little more is on offer in the way of food and evening entertainment.

★ Looking for a themed room? Well you're in the right place! Whether you want to be pirates or royalty, there's a room for that.

What Disney Won't Tell You

★ Depending on which bus stop you're closest too, you may have to wait for a couple of buses.

★ Moderate resorts are the larger resorts and so it may be a walk to the food locations, main pool etc.

★ Because of their popularity, availability at these resorts is few and far between in peak seasons.

★ Due to bodies of water, mosquitoes are a common irritant.

1. Disney's Fort Wilderness Cabins

This resort offers the magic of Disney but the escape of a wilderness campground. You can easily spend a chilled day here forgetting you're even in Walt Disney World. Fort Wilderness celebrates the classic American aesthetic you may have seen in The Parent Trap (1998).

Fort Wilderness is by far one of my favourite resorts. It's a great place to just enjoy time with friends/family. So even if you don't end up staying here, do stop-by for dinner or an afternoon of recreation. The resort offers some of the best 'beyond the parks' activities you'll find.

Why not take your little one on their very first pony ride, paddle a canoe down the bayou or take a wagon ride before you enjoy the Hoop-Dee-Doo Musical Revue. Hoop-Dee-Doo is great for a special occasion or to mix-up your holiday routine. It's a dinner show where you and your family get to feast on an all-you-care-to-enjoy (and drink) dinner whilst clapping, singing and laughing along to the country inspired show. Call +1 407-WDW-DINE to book.

If you can't afford the dinner show this time, be sure to go for dinner next-door at Trail's End. An all American buffet featuring pot roast, cowboy beans, corn bread and strawberry shortcake. If you're looking for a cheap evening, head to Chip and Dale's campfire. Here you can get a Smores pack to roast marshmallows by the fire ($10), sing and dance with Chip and Dale before enjoying a Disney movie on the big open air screen for FREE. There's so much to do here, you'll have to visit a number of times to see it all.

The cabins at Fort Wilderness offer you the benefit of being together, with the added perk of space. Cabins feature a kitchen, lounge and family bathroom. You'll have more than enough space to relax after a day in the parks.

BEST FOR	VALUE FOR MONEY	LOCATION

FUN FACT

Fort Wilderness was once home to Walt Disney World's first ever water park; River Country. Whilst the park closed in 2001 following the decline in tourism and the larger Typhoon Lagoon water park opening, the park sat abandoned for some 18 years before being demolished in 2019.

2. Disney's Port Orleans - Riverside

ADAM'S CHOICE - If there's one resort that is the best value for money, in my opinion it's Port Orleans - Riverside! Whilst not technically a deluxe resort, I always feel like it is one. For the amount it offers, matched with the level of theming and pure quality, it's really something special. You could even treat yourself to a Royal Guest Room for an extra magical stay. These themed accommodations offer a room that has been decorated for Disney royalty; kitted out with the subtleties that make it the most 'Disney' room you'll find at Walt Disney World.

PRO TIP

For more luxury at no extra cost, I recommend requesting one of the 'Magnolia Bend' buildings. Whilst still a standard room, their design is a bit more fancy.

Riverside hosts one of the best evening entertainments with the singing piano man on select nights each week. It has one of the best kid-friendly pools, as well as lots of quiet pools dotted around the resort. Additionally, you'll be able to use a boat service to Disney Springs for shopping and dining. My advice is to request a room close to the main area since it is a big resort. It'll make the walk to refill your resort mugs that much easier.

BEST FOR

VALUE FOR MONEY

LOCATION

3. Disney's Port Orleans - French Quarter

Sister resort to Port Orleans - Riverside, French Quarter offers a similar location in that it's close to Disney Springs and just a short walk from Riverside. This is actually the smallest resort on property, which has it's benefits and compromises. Whilst it's a favourite of families that are looking for that small-town vibe and the freedom to let the kids wander, the quick service is small and there is no table service dining here. There is however a jazz club and the infamous beignets served at Scatt Cat's Club Cafe.

The resort's design embodies the culture and architectural style of New Orleans. Whilst I believe you get more for your money over at Riverside, there's something to admire in the cobbled streets that make up the walkways around the resort. The resort is ideal for knowing your little ones are unlikely to lose their way back to the room, thanks to the resorts more compact layout.

BEST FOR	VALUE FOR MONEY	LOCATION
		✦ ✦ ✦ ✦ ✦

4. Disney's Caribbean Beach

If you've ever looked at booking via Virgin Holidays, you've probably seen that this resort comes up as the best price for a moderate resort. For that reason, it's British holiday-maker central! As it's so popular with us Brits, it'll normally fill up if there's a promotion going that applies to moderate resorts.

Whilst the Skyliner is a massive benefit of this resort (as it's the main transfer station for all three lines), there are some compromises. The merchandise and quick service are very small in comparison to the size of the resort and how many guests will utilise these spaces. I personally think you can get more for your money elsewhere (in terms of room design, food offerings etc.) but it is a fan favourite with many regular guests. Disney's Riviera Resort is located just next door, so there are some other dining options just a short walk away.

BEST FOR	VALUE FOR MONEY	LOCATION

5. Disney's Coronado Springs

Out of all the Disney hotels I've stayed at, this one exceeded my expectations the most. Having a similar layout to Caribbean Beach, I always assumed this would be the same… It isn't! The hispanic theme that runs throughout the resort is fantastic and the rooms are as if you're staying at a deluxe resort, without paying the price.

Since the addition of Gran Destino Tower in 2019 (improved lobby, tower rooms and additional dining), there's plenty of choice when it comes to eating and drinking at Coronado Springs. The pool is certainly one-of-a-kind and the amenities at this resort make it a close contender for 'Adam's choice.' This resort also benefits from being slap-bang in the middle of Disney property, so it doesn't take very long to get anywhere. All together, it's one of my favourite resorts.

BEST FOR	VALUE FOR MONEY	LOCATION

Deluxe Resorts

It's time for the best of the best! Now I warn you, if you're looking to stick to a strict budget, stop reading now. Disney knows what luxury looks like and they make sure it's priced accordingly.

If money's no object on your next Walt Disney World holiday or you're looking to make your trip something truly special, this is certainly the section for you. With above and beyond service standards, signature dining and rooms that'll make you question whether or not you're dreaming, you're sure to love staying at one of these hotels.

Benefits of Deluxe Hotels

★ Each deluxe resort is located next to one of the four theme parks (sometimes even walking distance).
★ Club Level (extra charge) offers you a step beyond just luxury with concierge service, complimentary snacks, drinks and private lounge.
★ Astounding resort theming.
★ Perfect for a romantic getaway or honeymoon.

What Disney Won't Tell You

★ They're very expensive! You'll often see the deluxe resorts on TV but not everyone can afford the high nightly room rate.
★ Whilst close to one park, they're often a long way from the others.
★ Unless you know what you're doing, you could pay a lot of money for a not-so-great room.
★ Expect to pay through the nose if you're looking for anything more than just a two queen room.

Club Level

If you're looking to upgrade your Walt Disney World stay even further, you may want to consider staying in a club level room. Currently, club level is available in all deluxe hotels, as well as Gran Destino Tower at Disney's Coronado Springs.

Club level is essentially a dedicated part of the hotel (normally a separate floor) that allows guests to have a more seamless check-in experience via a dedicated concierge desk, access to complimentary snacks and drinks throughout the day, turn down service and a concierge team that will go above and beyond to make your stay as magical as can be. Whilst you'll be paying a much higher nightly rate, these services do make your stay very special indeed.

Is it right for me?

I would only recommend paying for club level if you were looking to make a shorter stay extra special and you wanted to spend a lot of time in the resort. I personally don't see the value in spending so much extra per night for access to the food/drinks/service if you were going to be out in the parks for most of your stay. I'd say, this would be a great idea for a honeymoon trip.

Benefits of Club Level

 Private lounge for relaxing and dining.

 Dedicated concierge team to assist in getting you dining reservations, event tickets etc.

 Snacks and drinks (including alcohol) served most of the day.

 Truly exceptional service standards that will make it hard to go back to standard rooms.

1. Disney's Grand Floridian Resort & Spa - (Magic Kingdom Area)

If you're looking for the ultimate in Disney luxury or you want the best of the best in club level service, look no further than the Grand. This Victorian style resort boasts monorail service to Magic Kingdom (just one stop away) and boat service directly back from the Magic Kingdom. Whilst the price is a little out there, it sure is luxurious.

The Grand Floridian, for me, is the 'treat yourself' resort. So if you're looking to make your holiday extra-special, or you're planning your honeymoon; the eye watering price might just be worth it for you.

If you choose to upgrade to Club Level, my advice is to pay the extra to stay in the Main Building. The Main Building Club Level overlooks the lobby and allows you to enjoy the evening pianist from the comfort of your private lounge - with snacks and drinks on tap.

BEST FOR	VALUE FOR MONEY	LOCATION

2. Disney's Polynesian Village Resort - (Magic Kingdom Area)

Drift away to the elegant land of Polynesia. With the essence of Hawaii in it's theming and dining offerings, Disney's Polynesian Village has a great atmosphere about it. The resort boasts one of the best family style restaurants (Ohana) and is one of the only places outside of Magic Kingdom where you can get a refreshing Dole Whip. You may even get a lay when you check-in.

I know a number of families that make this their go-to because they enjoy spending so much time at the resort.

If you choose to stay here, my advice would be to request a room either close to the beach or main lobby. It's bigger than you think.

BEST FOR	VALUE FOR MONEY	LOCATION

FUN FACT

On Walt Disney World's opening day of October 1st 1971, Disney's Contemporary Resort was meant to be the first resort hotel to open alongside the Magic Kingdom. However, due to technical problems and delays with operations, The Polynesian Village actually ended up opening first.

3. Disney's Contemporary Resort - (Magic Kingdom Area)

Not every hotel has a monorail running through the atrium! If you've been to Walt Disney World before, there's very little chance you missed this hotel. Renowned for it's unique architecture and contemporary style, if you're looking for simplistic luxury, the Contemporary may be the place for you.

Having recently undergone an extensive refurbishment, the resort has had a new lease of life added to it. With rooms now themed to the Incredibles, a refreshed lobby and a new popular on-site signature restaurant called Steakhouse 71, there's a lot of new things to explore at this hotel.

I personally wouldn't recommend looking to stay here if you're on a strict budget. As the resort is very popular with long-time visitors and actually has very few rooms when compared to the other hotels, the price per night is often the most expensive on property.

Is it worth the high price tag? Not in my opinion. As the theme is very limited in order to maintain the Contemporary feel, I personally would rather pay the same money for one of the other Magic Kingdom resorts. Those that feel a bit more 'out there' in their design. However, for the best price, my advice is to book as far in advance as possible. Or, you can occasionally get a very last minute deal with seasonal 'room only' offers or annual pass discount.

BEST FOR

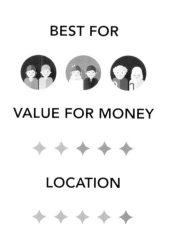

VALUE FOR MONEY

✦ ✦ ✦ ✦ ✦

LOCATION

✦ ✦ ✦ ✦ ✦

4. Disney's Wilderness Lodge - (Magic Kingdom Area)

If you love the idea of cuddling up in a cabin, high up the mountains; Wilderness Lodge may be the place for you. With a spectacular lobby and mountainous Americana inspiration, this resort is something truly special. Surrounded by gorgeous woodland, you can easily forget you're in central Florida.

This resort benefits from being close to Magic Kingdom, whilst allowing you to escape the hustle and bustle. Slightly off the beaten track, some people may find it a bit too secluded; but with a fantastic pool and lakeside bar & grill, I really love staying at this resort.

Rooms at Wilderness Lodge have recently been refurbished, but I wouldn't say they're to everyone's taste. One of the best things about this hotel, is that it's a consistently affordable deluxe option. For just a bit more than the price of a moderate, you could get access to being closer to Magic Kingdom and enjoy those Extended Evening Hours exclusive for deluxe hotel guests.

BEST FOR	VALUE FOR MONEY	LOCATION
👨‍👩‍👧 👩‍👧	✦ ✦ ✦ ✦ ✦	✦ ✦ ✦ ✦ ✦

5. Disney's Boardwalk Inn - (Epcot Area)

Are you a night owl? Well the Boardwalk is the place to be. Known for it's close proximity to Epcot via International Gateway (the back entrance) and it's vibrant nighttime scene, the Boardwalk uses a turn-of-the-century theme to make you feel as though you're staying along a Victorian pier.

This is also a great resort to visit for a look around. The Boardwalk has dining, entertainment and bars open till late. The pool is fun for kids with it's carnival theming and the rooms offer class, whilst also being playful. My only criticism with this resort; is that it charges more per night than other hotels with better theming and facilities in my opinion. E.g. neighbouring Yacht and Beach Club. I'd certainly say this is a more grown-up resort if you were thinking of staying here.

BEST FOR	VALUE FOR MONEY	LOCATION

✦ ✦ ✦ ✦ ✦   ✦ ✦ ✦ ✦ ✦

7. Disney's Yacht & Beach Club Resort - (Epcot Area)

ADAM'S CHOICE - Love swimming? Look no further than the Yacht and Beach Club. This twin hotel features the Yacht Club (themed to nautical luxury) and the Beach Club (themed to fun at the seaside); with both resorts sharing a water park! This is the only pool on property featuring a lazy river and sandy bottom. It has the tallest water slide out of all the on-site hotels, two hot tubs and more! If you enjoy the seaside and water, you'll be right at home here.

I personally prefer the Yacht Club resort for it's more mature offerings and styling. It has two luxury restaurants: Ale & Compass and one of my favourite on site restaurants; The Yachtsman Steakhouse. Beach Club does a great job of hosting families with their character buffet Cape May Cafe and the famous ice cream parlour; Beaches and Cream. Here your family could take on the 'Kitchen Sink Challenge.' Ordering a kitchen sink will have lights flashing and the cast members shouting as they bring over your 8 scoops of ice cream, every topping in the house and a whole can of whip cream (A WHOLE CAN?!).

BEST FOR	**VALUE FOR MONEY**	**LOCATION**

PRO TIP

When checking into your Disney resort, I recommend asking if they have any 'complimentary upgrades available'. Sometimes when there's relatively low occupancy, cast members may have the opportunity to reallocate your room with a better view. This of course isn't guaranteed, but can sometimes mean you get a little extra magic without paying anything more.

8. Disney's Animal Kingdom Lodge - (Animal Kingdom Area)

Escape to the savannahs of Africa at one of my favourite Walt Disney World resort hotels. Disney's Animal Kingdom Lodge offers you a destination resort whilst also being close to the fun of Animal Kingdom theme park. The resort is shaped like a horseshoe and surrounded by wide-open spaces for animals to roam freely passed your balcony.

Whilst you'll be compromising on being further away from other theme parks and Disney springs, in my opinion, the value for money definitely makes up for it. Not only that, you can feel like you've got an escape from the crowds and there's plenty to enjoy during a resort/pool day.

There's something about this resort that makes it stand out above the others for me. The food, the cast and the atmosphere is so transportive, it has another layer to it than just being a 'Disney' hotel. It creates magic in reality and not just in fantasy. Here, I can genuinely forget I'm in Florida and just enjoy the peaceful surroundings. If you don't end up staying here, I highly recommend visiting.

If you've stayed at a moderate resort before and you're looking to level up this trip, Animal Kingdom Lodge is a great affordable deluxe option. It's also a great place to stay for a longer trip when you're not in a rush to get it all done quickly.

BEST FOR

VALUE FOR MONEY

✦ ✦ ✦ ✦ ✦

LOCATION

✦ ✦ ✦ ✦ ✦

PRO TIP

Animal Kingdom Lodge is great for a first time deluxe stay, as it's more affordable when booking a standard view. If you do book this view, call and kindly request for a partial savannah view (it's included in this room rate).

Disney Vacation Club

Now, before I get started on Disney Vacation Club (DVC), I highly recommend that if you haven't been to Walt Disney World yet and you're planning your first trip (or first trip in a long time), just skip this part entirely. You would need to have a good understanding of what a Disney World holiday means to you and how often you're likely to visit, before even considering becoming a DVC member. At least, that's my advice.

What is Disney Vacation Club?

Disney don't like to call it a time-share, but it's essentially a time-share. By investing in the membership, you should in theory save on your future holidays.

The membership all works on a point system. When becoming a member, you choose how many points you'd like to buy. You will then get that number of points allocated to you every year, for the length of your membership. You can then use those points to book your accommodation at Disney. Still with me?

Home Resort

A DVC resort, is a dedicated collection of rooms/villas that are designed for members to use their points. Most of the deluxe resorts at Walt Disney World, have a DVC resort attached to them.

When you buy into the membership, you choose one of these DVC resorts to be your 'home resort.' This will determine the price of your membership when you buy in, the cost of your annual dues and how long your contract is. When a DVC resort is built, essentially a 50 year countdown starts. For example, if you bought into a resort that was built 20 years ago, you'd have a contract that would last 30 years.

Your home resort is also where you'll have priority in booking. You can book your home resort 11 months prior to your chosen check-in date. You're welcome to use your points at the other DVC resorts, however, you can only book as far as 7 months prior.

How much does it cost?

In essence, it depends. At the time of publishing, the minimum contract you can buy directly through Disney and get all the membership benefits (e.g. invitations to member events, merchandise/dining discounts, access to member lounges etc.) is 150 points.

If you buy into Grand Floridian, it's going to cost you more than say; Animal Kingdom Lodge. Grand Floridian has newer contracts, is a well located resort and is limited in availability. Animal Kingdom Lodge has more availability, isn't as well located and has less than 38 years left on contracts.

Should you buy directly through Disney, they'll share the 'price per point' for each resort and share any current discounts (for example, they'll sometimes discount points on new resorts to help them sell quicker). If we assume the current price per point at the resort you want is $200, a 150 point contract would cost you about $30,000 (plus contract closing costs and annual dues).

Now obviously, not everyone has $30,000+ lying around to pre-pay for their Disney holidays. With that in mind, most people will choose to finance this sum. If financing through Disney, you can choose a loan over 5 or 10 years.

Annual Dues

Whilst the actual cost of your membership is a one-time cost (whether financed or paid in cash), you will be required to pay annual dues each year. These will be billed in January and can be paid online via your DVC dashboard. Annual dues are calculated by number of points and the home resort. The more points you have and the more upkeep the resort requires, the more you'll pay in dues.

Who is DVC right for?

First things first, it's not right for everyone. Even for someone who travels to Walt Disney World as often as I do, it was no easy decision as to whether or not is was right for me.

I would recommend that if you plan on visiting Walt Disney World at least every other year, for the rest of your days and always staying on Disney property, it's worth looking into. However, there's a big consideration for whether or not it's affordable for you, the commitment it involves and if you can get the full use out of it.

Using Your Membership

In practice, it's all pretty seamless. On the DVC website, you just log-in to your membership, browse which resorts are available, book your stay depending on how many points you have and voilà!

When you check-in to your DVC resort, you won't have anything to pay. You can cancel a DVC stay, however, if you cancel less than 31 days prior to the check-in date, those points will go into 'holding.' These points then have to be used within the current 'use year' (the year those points were originally allocated to) and you can only use them when booking a trip less than 60 days in advance. So essentially, if you cancel last minute, you'll now have to book last minute.

You are also able to bank points in to next year and even borrow from the year ahead. So, say you wanted to have the trip to end all trips, you could save your points one year, pull from the year ahead and then end up with a stock-pile of points to splash out on a bigger villa for a longer time.

Renting DVC Points

If you're not a DVC member but you're interested in staying in a DVC villa, there are third-party sites that rent out DVC points. Basically, if a member doesn't want to use their points this year, they can organise through one of these third-party sites, for a cash paying guest to rent their points off them.

Similar to before, I recommend looking into these services yourself and seeing if they're right for you and your holiday. They may be a good way to try before you buy if you're thinking about DVC or potentially a way to save some money on your accommodation.

How many points would I need?

This is very much a 'how long is a piece of string' scenario. It will again depend on your personal budget, preferred home resort, size of villa you'd like to stay in, the frequency of your trips, the time of year etc.

A 150 point contract at Disney's Saratoga Springs for example, would comfortably get you 2 weeks in a deluxe studio in the low season every year. However, for a better idea, you can find the 'points charts' on the DVC website, that will help you see how many points the various room types cost throughout the year.

Buying DVC

Before you consider buying into the membership, it's important to do your own research, crunch the numbers, review your own personal circumstances and think about if this is really right for you. The information in this guide, is merely an overview.

You can either purchase directly through Disney, or on the resale market (again, I'd recommend researching which method is right for you).

Direct - If you choose to go direct, I recommend planning to start the process on your next holiday to Walt Disney World, or aboard Disney Cruise Line. Try and chat with one of the Disney Vacation Club guides dotted around the parks and schedule a tour at the DVC Preview Center. If you're staying on property, they'll arrange transportation to and from the center. If you want to go to the parks after your visit, they'll happily take you there for no charge.

At the center, you'll be set-up with a guide who will walk you through the membership, share more specific costs with you (e.g. closing costs and annual dues) and take you around some of the show rooms they have on-site. Disney aren't about a hard sell, but it's worth noting this is still very much a sales environment. Doing your research before this visit will ensure you ask the right questions.

Resale - If and when someone decides they no longer want their DVC contract/ membership, they may choose to list their contract on a resale site. These sites are not affiliated with Disney directly, but instead offer a space for buyers and sellers to exchange. Whilst resale can offer you some great deals in terms of price per point, buying resale doesn't get you the benefits of buying direct (e.g. discounts, exclusive events etc.).

Stand-Alone DVC Resorts

Whilst most DVC resorts are attached to an already established deluxe resort hotel, these properties are stand-alone DVC resorts. These are intended for DVC members to purchase contracts and use their points at. However, there is a limited amount of inventory made available for non-member/cash paying guests.

Benefits of these DVC Resorts

★ They offer more spacious accommodations that feature kitchenette's and washer/dryers.
★ Often more affordable to share a villa with a large family than it is to get several standard rooms in a deluxe resort.
★ Great resort theming.
★ More of a family vibe, since most people staying in these resorts have been multiple times to the same DVC resort.

What Disney Won't Tell You

★ Availability is few and far between as there's only a small allocation open for cash paying guests. Meaning, you'll most likely have to book far in advance.
★ Compared to similar layouts elsewhere on property (e.g. Art of Animation) these villas are very expensive for a cash reservation.
★ These resorts tend to be further away from the parks than standard deluxe resorts.

1. Disney's Saratoga Springs - (Disney Springs Area)

Similar to Old Key West below, Saratoga Springs is more for the repeat visitor that calls Saratoga home. The theme of this resort is carriages, horse stables and the like. For me, you can find much better theming for the same price elsewhere on property. However, if you want to spend a lot of time shopping and eating at Disney Springs, this is the only resort within walking distance. Also, if someone in your party is a big golfer, this is where you'll find a huge golf course to enjoy.

BEST FOR	VALUE FOR MONEY	LOCATION

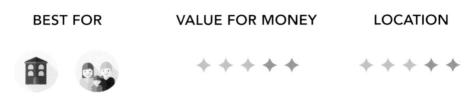

2. Disney's Old Key West - (Disney Springs Area)

Opened in 1991, this was the first DVC resort and has a very loyal following among it's contracted members. If you're looking for a more Florida feel, this is probably the resort for you. Guests most often say how much bigger the villas are here (due to their unique floor-plans) and what great value for money/points it is. Availability however, is often scarce because of the affordability aspect.

BEST FOR

VALUE FOR MONEY

LOCATION

3. Disney's Riviera Resort - (Epcot Area)

ADAM'S CHOICE - Welcome to my home resort! After much deliberation, I finally decided to take the plunge in becoming a Disney Vacation Club member and choosing Riviera as my home resort. For me, it was all about three things: location, location, location. The Skyliner connects you to Epcot and Hollywood Studios, whilst you're also equal distance from Animal Kingdom, Magic Kingdom and Disney Springs. Not to mention, this resort is so beautiful.

Disney are definitely looking to modernise their luxury styling and Riviera is a big step in the right direction. Mirroring the style of other five star resorts (e.g. Four Seasons), Riviera Resort is something unlike anything else on Disney property. I highly recommend visiting Topolino's Terrace on the top floor for an exceptional character breakfast or fine dining evening meal.

Inspired by Walt Disney's love of European architecture and the French Riviera, this new resort blends spectacular room design with elegant food from across the pond. This resort marks a new milestone in Disney's evolution of the Disney Vacation Club product, in creating a dedicated DVC resort that rivals some of the staple deluxe hotels across property.

BEST FOR	VALUE FOR MONEY	LOCATION
👨‍👩‍👧 👩‍👩	✦ ✦ ✦ ✦ ✦	✦ ✦ ✦ ✦ ✦

Off Property

Whilst I love staying on Disney property, it's sometimes a lot more affordable to stay off Disney property in a near-by hotel or villa. Likewise, with the benefits of staying at Disney depleting in recent years, off property accommodations are becoming more and more appealing.

Villa or Hotel?

My family and I have stayed in both villas and hotels. In my experience, the hotels have added much more value to our stays. Both with housekeeping, on-site dining and a reception team. However, sometimes a villa is a great way to have your own house for the length of your trip and feel like you're coming 'home' at the end of a long day in the parks. You will need a hire car though.

Tips for Staying in a Hotel

★ There are a multitude of hotels near Walt Disney World and thus the competition for price is always hot in the area. You're more likely to find a killer deal by choosing to stay in an off-site hotel if you book smartly.
★ Take a look at the included services and the location of the hotel. Free transport to the parks and being close to popular restaurants, are huge helps in making your off-site stay enjoyable.
★ If you choose an official neighbour hotel of Disney (e.g. the hotels in the Disney Springs area) you can still get access to some of the on-site perks like Early Entry to the theme parks, whilst still saving some money.
★ Hotels are notorious for having hidden charges (like resort fees). Do some digging and weigh up all the costs before choosing to book a good rate.

Tips for Staying in a Villa

⭐ If you're travelling with a large group, a villa may be the most affordable option if you're all wanting to stay together and are booking in advance.

⭐ Fresh food isn't always cheaper from the supermarket. Most fresh produce has to travel to Florida, so don't be surprised to find fresh meat, fruit and vegetables more expensive than going out for a meal.

⭐ Research the area. Just like anywhere, there are safer places than others. Whilst the price of a villa may be a steal, it's important to check where your villa will be. Your safety is something that can't be compromised for price.

Do Your Research!

Whether choosing to stay in a hotel or a villa, it's paramount that you do your research. Read reviews, check out the local area on Google Maps and find out how long it'll take for you to get to each park. The last thing you want is a 45+ minute drive back to your hotel/villa after a 10 hour day walking in the hot Florida sun.

Don't Tighten the Purse Strings Too Much

Whilst you're shopping hundreds of options, it's important to remember that not all hotels/villas will make for a dream holiday. Whether you think it or not, you will be spending a lot of time at your accommodation. One of my biggest tips is the need for rest time. You want to feel comfortable in wherever you choose to stay. For that reason, I wouldn't make my hotel or villa the first compromise if it came down to price. It may be one of the biggest costs but it could make or break your trip. I speak from experience when I say I've gone for the 'do the job' accommodation and instantly regretted it on arrival.

Chapter 3
WHICH TIME IS YOUR TIME?

When you consider Walt Disney World is open 365 days a year and there's an abundance of annual festivals and special events, it's sometimes difficult to decide when you'd like to go. Maybe you want the weather that suits your family's preferences or perhaps you're looking for the most affordable time of year?

I'm sorry to say that choosing your time to go is a never ending list of ifs and buts. Ultimately, it comes down to what your priorities are. That's how I've designed this part of Dream Guide. Start with your priority, whether that's being there for a special event, for the best weather, for the lowest crowds or for the cheapest time of year. I'll then share some advice on how best to narrow it down.

Choose the priority that's right for your travel party and turn to the relevant page. There I'll give you the best tips for your wants and needs.

WEATHER

Florida seems to work on two seasons rather than four. Winter and Summer. If you're travelling December - March, expect it to be chilly some days. Whilst it's unlikely you'll see frost, you'll still need a jacket with you. April - November is basically summer. Expect hot days and warm nights. Because of these two extremes, choosing to go in the transition period, means you're more likely to get some nice temperatures and less likely to encounter disruptive rain.

Don't worry about dates of travel just yet. We'll cross that bridge on the booking section. For now, just find a season you'd most likely enjoy planning your holiday for.

If you consult the graph on the right, you'll see when temperatures may be more to your liking. If I've rated a month 5 - beware it'll be very hot and very humid. If you're traveling from northern states in the US or the UK, chances are you won't mind the lower temperatures. However, temperatures in winter months can change day-by-day.

If you want to bake to a crisp, June - September is most definitely your time. On the next page, check out some of my best advice for the time of year you're considering with pros and cons.

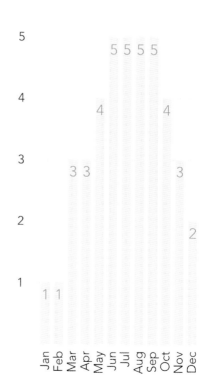

January - March

If the cold never bothered you anyway, you're looking at the right time of year. Not only that, you'll be able to take advantage of some slightly lower crowds compared to other times in the year.

Tips for January - March

★ If you love art and don't mind going as early as January, check dates for Epcot's Festival of the Arts. You'll have the chance to step into artwork and try food & drinks that have a special artistic flair to them.

★ To all the runner's out there, you may wish to participate in a Run Disney event held in this period. These events feature a 5k, 10k, half marathon and full marathon. Registrations sell out quickly, so plan ahead if this is your thing.

★ Look out for dates of Epcot's Flower & Garden festival. Typically starting towards the end of February, this festival features multiple speciality food stalls, beautiful character topiaries and colourful gardens everywhere.

★ Spring break is the second busiest time of year at Walt Disney World. Whilst Spring Break dates vary per each state, check school holidays for states within driving distance of Florida. This is when the resort will be busiest.

Pros for January - March

★ There's fewer people in the parks compared to other times of year.
★ Great Epcot events throughout the season (check Disney's website for up-to-date information & dates).
★ Thanks to less demand, you can get some great deals during these months.

Cons for January - March

★ The parks often prioritise repairs and construction during this time. Don't be surprised if there's a crane topping up paint on Cinderella's castle.
★ Watch out for Feb/March as this is the start of Spring Break season. It's very busy during this period.
★ It can be bloomin' cold.

April - June

This is possibly the best time of year for goldilocks weather! Not so hot your shoes melt into the asphalt but not so cold you'll need to bring a coat. I've found the best weather during April and May specifically.

Tips for April - June

★ Especially in April/May, this is one of the rare times in the year that you can enjoy the heat without the humidity. This nice weather is no secret however, so expect it to be reasonably busy around the Easter holidays.
★ May is a good time for experiencing the parks at their best in my opinion. Reasonable crowds, nice weather and some pretty good deals normally.
★ It's around this time of year Disney will open their new attractions and shows.

Pros for April - June

★ Perhaps the best weather out of the entire year.
★ As the parks prepare for their busiest season, you'll often find most attractions are free from routine refurbishment.
★ If you avoid the national and local holidays, it's often not too busy.

Cons for April - June

★ With Easter and a number of national holidays in these months, it's tricky to dodge all busy times.
★ Schools in the US tend to break-up for summer around May-June, so the crowds will pick-up.
★ Prices will be higher around national and local holidays.

July - September

It's getting hot in here! Summer is in full swing during these months and I warn you now, it's not for the faint hearted. With temperatures often exceeding 32c (90f), 100% humidity on most days and thunderstorms as routine as the 3 o'clock parade, it's not the most comfortable time of year when it comes to weather.

Not only is the weather sometimes torture, US and UK schools are out for summer which makes the parks consistently busy and the prices for hotels and park tickets go up significantly.

Tips for July - September

- ★ Whilst Summer is no longer the 'busiest' time, it's still not quiet. Pack your patience for wait times.
- ★ When booking for these months, either book 12+ months in advance or last minute.
- ★ Be prepared for extreme weather and insure your trip against cancellations due to hurricanes.

Pros for July - September

- ★ June is normally the month new attractions will aim to open by. As such, you could be one of the first people to experience the latest addition to Walt Disney World.
- ★ Late August/early September, is now one of the quietest times of year in Walt Disney World.

Cons for July - September

- ★ It's hot! Very hot!
- ★ On-the-day park tickets are priced based on how busy the season is. If you're travelling domestically within the US, be prepared for these prices.
- ★ Regular thunderstorms will cause some attractions to close often.
- ★ Did I mention it's hot?

October - December

This is the season for more events than you can shake a stick at. With Mickey's Not So Scary Halloween Party, Epcot's Food & Wine Festival, Mickey's Very Merry Christmas Party and Epcot's Festival of the Holidays all in this season, there's more than enough to make your visit during these months something extra special. These months are great if you've been to Disney before and you're now looking for something to make this trip different from the last.

Tips for October - December

★ Florida's hurricane season runs until November. Insure your trip and be ready for hurricane disruption.

★ Book special ticketed events ASAP. These events can sell out quickly.

★ Dodge the major holidays to avoid spending more than you bargained for. You can also find some sweet spots that aren't too busy.

Pros for October - December

★ The weather is a little kinder day to day (temperature wise).

★ There will always be something special to do. Whether it's Halloween or Christmas, you'll be incredibly entertained (for a price).

★ You'll likely get the chance to see some amazing fireworks.

Cons for October - December

★ Christmas is the busiest time of year for Walt Disney World. Don't be too surprised if most resorts are sold out. Book in advance to avoid being disappointed.

★ If you time it wrong, you could be in for an incredibly busy time.

PRICE

Money, money, money. It makes the world go round and unfortunately, a lot of what we plan for our Walt Disney World holidays is based on our budget. It's pretty common for price to be the biggest priority in making a trip to Disney viable. As I go to Walt Disney World more often than the typical family, I've learnt a thing or two about making a trip affordable. From how/where/when you book, through to saving whilst on your trip, hopefully I can save you a pretty penny.

The Cheapest Time to Go

Let's not beat around the bush here; the cheapest time to visit Walt Disney World is late January through to mid February. As the weather is typically colder and people have less money after the holidays, this tends to be when Disney will offer discounts to keep rooms occupied. If you can A: be flexible enough to go during this time, B: don't mind it being cold, C: won't miss a couple of rides being closed for refurbishment and D: can avoid the national holidays, you could get a great deal!

Whilst winter may be the cheapest time of year, it's not ideal for everyone. For that reason, I'll take you through some dos and don'ts when it comes to prioritising price for your holiday. It's not practical for me to put prices in Dream Guide as they'll likely be out of date by the time it goes to print. For that reason, use my tips to choose your ideal time based on current availability and pricing.

Best Price Realisations

If you're looking to go to Walt Disney World for as cheap as possible, there are some harsh realities I have to impart.

- ★ You cannot go to Walt Disney World during the school breaks cheaply. If you've got a little one and you need to go outside of term time, your best bet is a half-term break when the American schools are likely still in session.
- ★ It's a gamble getting a good deal on a holiday like this. You need to have a little faith (trust and pixie dust) that when you find a good price, it's worth the leap of faith to book when you see it. If you wait a day or two, things will likely change and it may be gone.
- ★ You might have to make some difficult compromises to get the trip within your budget. Whether that's the hotel, flight or that day at Universal, it may not be possible to do everything you wanted to on this particular trip.
- ★ If this is your first time going, consider a time when there are no big holidays. That way, you get to see the resort as a blank canvas. You'll save a little money and give yourself something to do next time to make it different.
- ★ Someone else may be able to get a better price than you. As stubborn as I am in trying to find the best price, sometimes a tour operator or travel agent can access special rates and beat what I've found. So it's worth checking.

PRO TIP

If you want to get your holiday for the best price and still travel in high season (e.g. Christmas), try and hold out booking until closer to the time. About 90-30 days before your intended arrival, you can find some discounted prices on flights and hotels as the resorts try to secure their occupancy going into high season. The only problem is that there is no guarantee your preferred hotel (or any) will have availability. Just be sure to check often.

First Holiday on a Budget

If you're dreaming of your first trip to Walt Disney World and you're on a tight budget, don't be too quick to book something that just happens to be in your price range. Do your research and make sure it's a resort you'll enjoy. Also, check what the additional costs may be (e.g. parking & tickets). Your first time needs to be magical and something like bad accommodation, can easily ruin the trip.

Book Ahead and Save

For most people, the most affordable way to book a Walt Disney World holiday (especially the first one) is to book over a year in advance during an offer. About Spring time, Disney tends to release an offer if you're booking for next year (e.g. booking 2024 in spring 2023). This could be anything from free nights to free dining. The great thing is, you'll only have to pay a deposit, and then you've got time to pay it off. It could make a very expensive trip more doable.

Room Only Discounts

Whilst UK offers come and go, Disney is pretty good at routinely offering room only discounts. The best way to find out about these, is to call the US booking line (+1 407-939 7829). Whilst you'll need to pay in dollars (and subsequently any exchange fees), this can end up being cheaper than booking the same room with a UK seller. Whilst the US phone agent may offer you packages with tickets and/or dining, these will almost always be cheaper booking UK side. So it's important to insist you'd like a room only quote. Room only bookings also only require a one night deposit, with the rest paid at check-in. They can also be cancelled with a full refund of deposit, just five days prior to check-in. A great option if you need some extra flexibility with your accommodation.

CROWDS

There's a common myth that there are quiet times to go to Walt Disney World. Well, I'm sorry to be the bearer of bad news but this just isn't the case. Not at a specific time anyway. Walt Disney World is the most visited tourist attraction in the world and so you're unlikely to find a time when you can walk on every attraction. However, there are times you can avoid to ensure you're not waiting over an hour for every attraction during your trip.

Typically, the rule of thumb is to avoid the American national holidays. Any times like Spring Break, Easter, Labor Day, Thanksgiving, Christmas or New Years Eve, draw in the largest crowds. It's also around these times you'll often see the highest prices. Why would you want to pay more for your holiday and get on fewer attractions? Especially if it's your first time visiting the resort? As such, if it's your first time, consider a break that may avoid these peak times.

PRO TIP

If you end up in a park and it's busy, stick to the right hand side of the walkways, as most Americans instinctively walk on the right. With this, you'll make more progress walking with the tide. When it comes to lines (e.g. quick service restaurants, security etc.) choose the line furthest away and check how dense the line is and whether there's lots of large families. Larger families take longer to organise/order, thus slowing down the line.

To help give you a better visual of the crowd levels throughout the year, I've created the following chart. This is a rough guide and should be treated as such, as dates and days of holidays change year on year. Each period has been ranked from 1 to 5 to show how busy it's likely to be. 1 being the quietest and 5 being the busiest. Just note: 1 doesn't mean everything's going to be a short wait time.

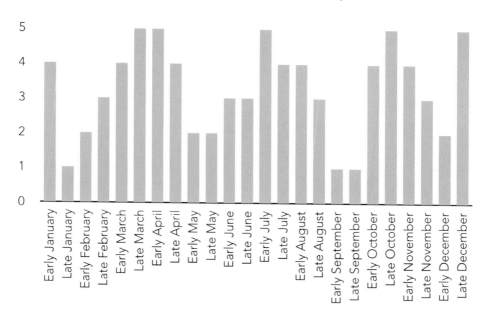

EVENTS

Walt Disney World knows how to celebrate! If you're looking for the ultimate Halloween party or maybe you're just looking for something to make your next holiday different from the last, Disney has you covered. Throughout the year, Disney hosts a variety of events that cater for many different interests. Whilst the dates of these events change year-on-year, I've done my best to let you know when they are and what they entail.

New Year's Eve

If you're looking to ring in the New Year with a bang, know that Magic Kingdom, Epcot and Hollywood Studios all like to put on a pretty spectacular celebration. Whilst it's the single busiest night of the year for all the parks, these firework shows are something to be marvelled! Epcot tends to be my go-to.

PRO TIP

If you're visiting over New Year's, Magic Kingdom will do a 'dress rehearsal' of their New Year's fireworks on December 30th. A good way to see the fireworks with fewer crowds.

Valentine's Day

If you happen to be in Magic Kingdom on Valentine's day, you may have the chance to enjoy some extra cute additions to Magic Kingdom. In years gone by, we've seen special meet and greets for the princesses to meet guests alongside their princes, decorations and themed treats.

Epcot's Flower & Garden Festival

Running through most of spring, Epcot transforms into a gardener's paradise. With extravagant flower beds and impressive topiaries, the park doesn't get much prettier than this. Not only that, you'll find a variety of food and drink kiosks around the World Showcase.

Easter

If your little ones (or you for that matter) would love the chance to meet the Easter Bunny, head to Magic Kingdom on Easter weekend. The daytime parade features a special Easter pre-parade featuring Mr & Mrs Easter Bunny and a flurry of Easter inspired costumes. There's also some Easter themed fun, often in the way of meet & greets.

Festival of the Arts

Hosted typically from the middle of January till early February, Festival of the Arts is an event that takes over Epcot. During this event little ones can enjoy arts and crafts events, there are art themed seminars, artistic food, drinks and photo opportunities. Not to mention lots of art to buy.

4th of July

Whilst a little awkward for us Brits, this is the day that Americans celebrate their independence. 4th of July is celebrated by the mother of all firework displays in Magic Kingdom. As this firework display doesn't typically feature projections, I recommend watching them from anywhere in the park but Main Street and the main hub in front of the castle.

Epcot's Food & Wine Festival

Typically running from September through to November, the festival brings a plethora of food and drink stalls to Epcot that allow you to taste your way (or roll your way) around the world. You'll find things you've never even heard of before and maybe see a band from way back when.

Mickey's Not So Scary Halloween Party - (ticketed event)

With event dates starting as early as August, this ticketed event turns Magic Kingdom into an exclusive Halloween party featuring a special stage show, Halloween parade and an awesome firework display. You can even dress up and go trick or treating.

Mickey's Very Merry Christmas Party - (ticketed event)

Christmas is one of my favourite seasons to visit Walt Disney World. At this special ticketed event, Magic Kingdom features a special stage show, complimentary cookies, the ultimate Christmas parade and a firework display that'll warm the heart of even the biggest Scrooge.

Epcot's Festival of the Holidays

Just in case you thought Epcot was lacking in festivals, there's more! During this event there'll be a special candlelight procession hosted by some pretty big names, beautiful decorations and the chance to hear each country's local holiday story. You could even meet Mr & Mrs Clause.

Run Disney Events

Throughout the year, Disney will host themed Run Disney events. These are typically held during the lower seasons when it's not too hot (e.g. January, February and April). These events allow runners to run through the parks and around Walt Disney World property. There's also exclusive merchandise, rare character appearances and cast members cheering you on. Registration for these events does sell out and they are not the cheapest running event you'll ever partake in. However, it's a very unique experience being able to run through Disney parks and you even get a medal at the end!

SCHOOL BREAKS

If you're travelling with a little one, chances are you'll have difficulty going outside of school holidays. For this reason, let me give you my advice for going during these breaks. Please note: this section will be in a UK format but should be a basic guide for other territories.

February Half-Term

If you're looking for a cheap getaway, this break could be perfect for you. Just note that by only going for a week, you'll likely have a more hectic schedule. Don't forget the kids will need to go back to school almost straight after your return. If you can, give them a couple days to recover.

Easter Holiday

Whilst you're likely to cross over with Spring Break, the weather is much more bearable during this period. Depending on the year, you may just avoid the worst of it. You'll likely be able to find a reasonable deal if you book far enough in advance. Just be prepared for some busy days here and there.

Spring Half-Term

Providing it falls at the end of May, this will hopefully be the very best school break to take your little ones to Disney. Whilst restricted to one week, the crowds are moderate and you'll likely visit before the heat gets too much. This can also end up being a little sweet spot with low crowds, good weather and lower costs.

Summer Holiday

Things have changed in recent years that have made Summer a better time to visit than others. Summer used to be the time to avoid and October - December was coined as the best for weather/low crowds. As such, a lot of visitors have moved to booking this time of year; leaving summer more enjoyable than previously. However, prices will typically still be high and it will be hot (very hot).

If you're restricted to this break, go as early as you can. August and September are excruciatingly hot and have the most thunder storms. If your child maybe finishes before the majority of other schools (e.g. they finish their exams early) you can get a not-so-bad deal and avoid the worst of the heat. However, if it's as quiet as possible you're looking for and you can handle the humidity, leave it as late as you possibly can as American schools go back in mid-August.

Autumn Half-Term

If you want better weather and the chance to experience Mickey's Not So Scary Halloween Party, this is the season for you. Just note however, the parks are considerably busier during this season. Non-party days at Magic Kingdom now have a reputation for being unbearably busy.

Christmas Break

Christmas in Disney is beautiful with a certain charm in the air (amongst the high crowds). Unless you can time your trip toward the beginning of December, I certainly wouldn't recommend the weeks around/over Christmas for a beginner. If you've done everything before though and know what you're in for, it might be a good time for you to visit. Just pack for hot and cold weather.

Chapter 4
BOOK THE MAGIC

Now you've got an idea of what your holiday may look like, it's time to start making these dreams a reality. Hopefully by this point you've highlighted a hotel or two and you've got an idea of when you'd like to visit.

In this chapter, I'm going to walk you through the different booking methods to help you get everything you need, everything you want and for the best price you can. There are no rules when it comes to booking your holiday. Some people like the comfort of booking a package and others are happy to book everything separately. However, I'll cover it all so you can book how you'd prefer.

Before I get into showing you how to book, let's run over some 'need to knows.' These will help you understand the different elements to a booking, what you do after you've booked and some of things that you'll need to learn for your trip.

If this is your first trip to Disney, there's a lot of words and terminology that's floating about. Until now, you may not have understood them. Before you start using the booking methods and part with your cash, it's important to know what you want and what you don't. The last thing you want is to say yes to something you don't need and paying the price for it (literally).

DISNEY DINING PLANS

In short - it's a way to pre-pay for your meals and save between 5-10% over the course of your holiday (depending on whether you use it to the max or not).

However, don't get distracted by that discount. Disney Dining Plans (of which there's a few) are something you need to understand before adding one to your trip. The last thing you want is to actually have lost money by the end of your holiday.

How does the dining plan work?

When you book a Disney resort hotel and park tickets together, you'll be eligible to add a dining plan to your package. It's an all or nothing system. You either have the dining plan for everyone in your travel party for every night of your stay, or not at all.

If you add a Dining Plan to your booking, you'll be allotted a number of dining credits (determined by the dining plan you choose) that you can use however you like throughout your holiday.

As a heads up, one of the plans is literally called 'Disney Dining Plan'. This may be referred to as the Table Service Dining Plan by some and is considered the main option. If you booked the 'Disney Dining Plan', you'd be allotted the following number of credits per person, per night of stay:

1 x Quick Service Meal (counter service)
1 x Table Service Meal (waiter service)
2 x Snacks (most food items around $5.00, illustrated by a logo shown on menus)

Disney will tell you exactly which locations accept the dining plan but it's pretty much all of them. With a plan, you'll be given a re-fillable resort mug and be free to use your credits as you wish. At a quick service meal, you'll typically be able to get a meal and a drink. You'll scan your magic band and be given a receipt with a zero balance.

At a table service meal, you get one main course, one dessert and one drink (some alcohol is included for adults over 21 years of age). Anything you order outside of this allotment will need to be paid for at the end of your meal. You'll simply scan your MagicBand, sign a receipt and be given the opportunity to tip your server. You can pay your tip in cash or charge it to your room.

Is a Disney Dining Plan right for you?

There's a number of things to consider when it comes to choosing whether or not you'd like a dining plan. However, there's a rule of thumb I like to use.

Let's say you booked a dining plan, but chose to spend two or three days outside of Disney eating. Maybe you go to Universal Studios, the Florida Mall or even somewhere like Olive Garden. If you didn't use three table service credits and three quick service credits, you've wasted about $240 per person.

If you're planning on spending almost every day of your Walt Disney World stay in Disney and eating in Disney, then the dining plan may be right for you.

However, it also depends on how much you and your family eat/drink. In my experience, if you're likely to have a cocktail, beer or glass of wine with every meal on holiday, the Dining plan is a great option. If you don't drink alcohol and you're not big on snacking throughout the day, in my experience, you'd be better off paying as you go.

What's included in a Dining Plan?

How much you get per person and per night of stay, is dependant on the dining plan you choose. The below chart describes how many dining credits each guest gets per night of stay.

Notice: At the time of this book going to print, Disney Dining Plans are temporarily unavailable. Please keep in mind that some of this information may change upon their return.

	Quick Service Dining Plan	Disney Dining Plan	Disney Dining Plan +	Deluxe Dining Plan
Re-Fillable Resort Mug	Length of Stay	Length of Stay	Length of Stay	Length of Stay
Snacks	2	2	2	2
Quick Service Meals	2	1	-	-
Table Service Meals	-	1	2	-
Choice of Quick Service, Table Service or Signature Restaurants	-	-	-	3

Get the Most Out of a Dining Plan

I mentioned you could save 5-10% earlier. However, you'll only save that amount if you use your dining plan in full and wisely. If you don't use all your credits, you may as well have given Disney a stack of cash for no reason.

Not only is it important to use all your credits but it can also depend on where you choose to dine. Whilst most options will be priced similarly, there are places where you wouldn't get your money's worth. If your meal at a quick service will cost less than $15 per person, consider another option to get the best value for the cost of the plan. Likewise, if you're dining at a table service restaurant, choosing the cheapest thing on the menu every time and only getting soft drinks, you'd have been better off paying as you went. Just be mindful is all I suggest.

Tips for Using a Dining Plan

⭐ **Make Reservations** (where applicable) - if on the Disney Dining Plan or Deluxe Dining Plan, I strongly recommend booking a restaurant for each day/night of your stay. You can cancel them the day prior if you think you're unlikely to go (and avoid the $10 per person no-show fee) but when you're committing to a dining plan, it's a good idea to have something booked. Not having reservations may result in lots of waiting and/or disappointment.

⭐ **Play the Signature Game** - On the Disney Dining Plan, there are a select number of table-service restaurants that will take two credits per person. More often than not, these are Disney's 'signature dining' restaurants (places like Jiko, Be Our Guest and Topolino's Terrace). If you chose to dine off-property one evening (e.g. the mall or Universal Studios), you can use that saved credit to now dine at a signature restaurant. This is a great way to try the fanciest restaurants on property without paying the higher price of the Deluxe Dining Plan.

⭐ **Tips** - When booking a dining plan, it's nice to get in the mindset of having everything paid for. However, your plan doesn't cover server tips. It's worth keeping that in mind when you come to budgeting your spending money.

- ★ **Splitting Credits** - Disney do allow you to split certain credits into other types of credit. Whilst what you can get for splits changes, you could quite easily split a quick service credit into snack credits. Chat to the front-desk for confirmation on splits.

- ★ **Use Your Snack Credits** - If come the end of your trip you have snack credits left over, head to your resort merchandise location to stock up on treats that'll last the trip home (e.g. rice krispie treats). They can also double up as gifts for friends and family back home.

OFFERS

When it comes to booking a Walt Disney World holiday, there aren't really any offers that will make your holiday 'cheap.' However, there are options that'll allow you to get more for your money.

- ★ **Free Dining** - By far one of the best deals Disney has offered in the past. Previously available during select months, Disney will allow you to get free breakfast with a value resort reservation, Quick Service Dining Plan with a moderate resort reservation and the Disney Dining Plan with a deluxe resort. Act fast if this offer makes a comeback, as it's extremely popular.

- ★ **UK Exclusive** - Disney knows that UK visitors have more to pay in airfare and as such, UK residents can benefit from cheaper park tickets, earlier access to room availability and more. Check Disney's website for the latest.

TICKETS

It's worth letting you know ahead of time, this is going to be a big cost of your holiday. There are a few options for purchasing theme park and water park tickets, which will depend on how you're booking and how many times you'd like to visit the parks.

If you're planning on spending anything less than five days in the Disney parks, you may be better off buying tickets through a US based certified seller (such as *Undercover Tourist*). With these sellers, you can save about 10% by purchasing day tickets in advance online. I would always discourage you from buying tickets at the park entrances, as this is by far the most expensive way to buy tickets.

However, anything over five days, you're best option is a 7 or 14 day ticket through Disney's website or through your travel agent (UK only). Traditionally, Disney have allowed British guests to buy 14 days for the price of 7. This is by far the best deal you can get for park tickets and will typically include Disney's water parks and the memory maker photo package (prices vary by season).

Once you've purchased your tickets, it may take up to 7 days for the ticket numbers to be issued. With this in mind, plan ahead to make sure you've bought your tickets with plenty of time before your trip. With those ticket numbers, you'll be able to link them to your My Disney Experience account...

Change: UK 7 and 14 day tickets are now priced according to season. Whilst they're still the best deal, the peak season prices are much more expensive than they used to be.

MY DISNEY EXPERIENCE

The biggest mistake guests make before a Walt Disney World holiday, is not using and not familiarising themselves with My Disney Experience (MDE). It's a free app and area of the Walt Disney World website that enables you to plan and manage your Walt Disney World holiday.

Available via the Apple App Store and GooglePlay store, I highly recommend downloading the app at least 60 days prior to departure. As mentioned above, there is a website version if you don't have a smart phone or tablet. Here, I'm going to explain what MDE is and how to utilise it before and during your trip.

What is My Disney Experience?

MDE is a one-stop-shop for all your Walt Disney World holiday needs. It's not that you can use it, but that you must use it.

Within the app and online, you'll be able to link your Disney hotel reservation, link your park tickets, book dining, browse park maps and check park opening times prior to your arrival. On your trip, you'll be able to check wait times for attractions, order food, check-in to your reservations, pay for merchandise, view your photos and purchase priority access to the popular theme parks attractions.

It's only by having a Disney account and using MDE, that you'll be able to get the most out of your trip. Not to mention enabling you to use your MagicBands and/or Key to the World Cards.

Can You Get Away with Not Using it?

In my opinion, no. Not using it will likely mean you miss out on the meals you want, waiting in lines you don't need to and being a step behind other guests.

Is it Difficult to Use?

Whilst not difficult, there are some tips and tricks to using MDE wisely. I'll give you the basics but Disney also provide a help desk and tutorials online.

Linking Your Information

When you first get started on MDE (in the app or online), you'll need to start by creating a Disney account if you don't already have one. Once signed in, you'll then need to go to the 'Friends & Family' section. Here you can add a profile for everyone that's going on your trip (yourself included). You can then link the park tickets you've purchased and assign these to each member of your party. This will allow you to use any MagicBands/Key to the World Cards to access the theme parks.

If you're staying in a Disney resort hotel, be sure to link your hotel reservation. This will make sure My Disney Experience knows you're an on-site guest. This will help you when coming to book your dining reservations, Park Passes and more.

I Need Help!

Disney has a collection of tutorials and FAQs on their website related to getting started with MDE. If you need to call the help desk, my advice is to call the moment they open in the US. This is currently 1pm (UK time). Otherwise, you may be waiting a while.

Park Pass Reservations

In order to access any Disney theme park on any given day, everyone in your party must have a free Park Pass Reservation, alongside a valid ticket. Essentially, you have to book your spot in each of the theme parks for each day of your trip.

Whilst this system was implemented during the pandemic to manage crowd levels, Park Pass Reservations are here to stay. The easiest way to make your reservations is via the Park Pass tab on the Walt Disney World website under the My Disney Experience section. You'll need to make sure your theme park tickets (and any Disney hotel reservations) have been linked to your account.

Park Pass availability depends on the type of guest you are. There are three categories:

⭐ **Resort Guest** - Staying in a Disney resort hotel or partnered hotel.
⭐ **Day Guest** - Staying off-property.
⭐ **Annual Pass Holders**

Resort guests tend to get more availability over the other categories.

If you're planning a last minute trip or you're visiting during a busy season (e.g. Christmas), it's important to check there's Park Pass availability before booking anything. You can check the availability calendars via the Park Pass tab online.

Some other things to note:

⭐ Park Passes can be cancelled at any time without charge.
⭐ If you're planning on park-hopping, you won't need a Park Pass for every park that day, just the first park you're planning on visiting (page 177).
⭐ Park Passes can be booked as soon as you've got your tickets sorted, right up until on the day (providing there's availability for your chosen park).
⭐ Park Passes are not required for the water parks.

Dining Reservations

Restaurants are currently available to book 60 days prior. Most restaurants have changing availability, but for popular locations like Cinderella's Royal Table, you'll need to book as soon as reservations are open. You can make dining reservations on the website via the 'Things to do' tab, or within the app.

If you're staying in a Disney resort hotel and you've linked your reservation to My Disney Experience, you'll be able to book restaurants for the length of your stay, 60 days prior to your check-in date. If you're staying off property, you'll need to book each day of your trip, 60 days prior. The system opens at 5:45am EST (10:45am in the UK), so I'd recommend setting calendar reminders to make sure you're ready to book at this time.

⭐ **Fees and cancellations** - Most restaurants are free to book. However, some may require you to pay in advance (e.g. Victoria & Albert's). Should you not turn up to a reservation, there's a $10 per person no-show fee. If you know you're not going to make a booking, cancel or modify it the day before to avoid getting charged the no-show fee. If something happens on the day out of your control, call the dining reservation line as they may be able to waive the fee in certain situations.

⭐ **Book as you go** - Because of the cancellation policy, a lot of people (and I mean a lot) will be cancelling reservations they have for the next day. This means that you can often book some amazing restaurants during your trip. Even those that are highly sought after will pop-up during your stay. Be sure to check the app at least once a day to see what's available. In my experience, the best time to check is first thing in the morning (before 6:30am).

★ **Check back** - The dining reservation system works on live availability. Meaning, if someone cancels their reservation or the system is holding a time for someone to book and they fail to complete, that time will become available again. If for any reason you didn't manage to get the reservation you wanted, check back and refresh the page a few times. Guests like to change their plans often, so you may just get lucky.

Mobile Order

Disney now encourages all guests to order quick service meals/snacks via Mobile Order. This service allows you to pre-order your quick service meals and then collect them within a certain time at a dedicated window.

The service has been much improved over the past couple of years and is now incredibly efficient (if you know how to use it correctly). Whilst one or two stand-by lines remain available for cash transactions, I would recommend using Mobile Order wherever you can. The stand-by lines move very slowly.

You can access Mobile Order via the My Disney Experience app. Before beginning an order, you'll be prompted to select a collection time. This may be from 'now' or you may have to choose a time in the future if there's a wait.

As collection times can fill up, my advice is to place your Mobile Order at least 2-3 hours ahead of time. That way, you'll ensure you've secured a return time that works well for your day. The last thing you want to hear is 'I'm hungry!', check the app, and realise the next return time is over an hour away...

When you arrive during your chosen window, you'll simply open your order within the app and click the 'I'm here, prepare my order' button. After a few minutes, the app will notify you that your order is ready for collection and which pick-up point to go to. It's worth noting, you can only enter the location/pick-up line, once you've reached this final screen. You then share your order number with the cast member at the window, and you're done!

Park Maps

Within the app, you can now see exactly where you are in the parks and how to get to where you'd like to go. Not only that, you can view approximate wait times for attractions, dining options, show times for entertainment and more.

Opening Times

Online and in the app, you can review opening times for the parks, as well as Early Entry and Extended Evening hours. These are typically made available approximately 90 days in advance.

Bus Times

If you're staying in a Disney resort, tap on the 'Resort Hotel' button within the app and this will open up the details relating to your stay. Within this section, is a Bus Times button. Tapping this will open up estimated wait times for the next bus to the four theme parks and Disney Springs. This is especially helpful when deciding when to leave your room.

DISNEY GENIE

Disney Genie is a new addition to the already established My Disney Experience app. This will only come into play when you're actually in Disney World. However, it's a good idea to wrap your head around it before you book your trip, to see if you may wish to utilise the paid elements of the service and budget accordingly.

Lightning Lanes

Before I get into the elements of Disney Genie, it's important to understand what a Lightning Lane is. Formerly know as the FastPass line, this is a physical line that allows you to bypass the main stand-by line for the majority of attractions.

What are the three elements of Disney Genie?

⭐ **1. Disney Genie** - Open to all guests, this is a free tool that allows you to select some preferences of what you'd like to do during your day. Disney Genie will then create a custom itinerary which recommends attractions, dining and entertainment for you. You're not required to use this.

⭐ **2. Disney Genie+** - This is a paid for service that allows you to book access to Lightning Lanes at most theme park attractions for one day. Using this service should mean you spend less time waiting in stand-by lines.

⭐ **3. Individual Attraction Selections** - Some of the most popular attractions are not covered by Disney Genie+. Individual Attraction Selections allow you to purchase a single Lightning Lane use, to one of these popular attractions. You do not need to pay for Genie+ in order to buy Individual Attraction Selections. These are simply a single purchase, to skip one stand-by line.

How much does Disney Genie+ cost?

If you're purchasing Disney Genie+ on the day, it's $15 (+tax) per person. However, if you're purchasing a 7 or 14 day UK ticket, you are able to add-on Disney Genie+ for the length of your ticket. On a 7 day ticket, this is £10.99 per person, per day. On a 14 day ticket, this is reduced to £6.99 per person, per day.

Costs are accurate at time of print, but subject to change in future.

How do you buy and use Disney Genie+?

You're welcome to purchase Disney Genie+ anytime from 00:01am for use on the same day, via the app. Alternatively, if you've purchased the length of ticket add-on, it'll already be active and ready to use alongside your park tickets.

From 07:00am, guests with Disney Genie+ will be able to go to the 'Tip Board' within the My Disney Experience app and book their first Lightning Lane return time. This is the same whether you're staying on or off property. It's important to note, the available time shown is simply the next available slot, and you cannot choose from a selection of return times. In booking a return time, act quickly. The time may change in the seconds it takes for you to select your party and confirm.

To redeem your Lightning Lane return time, just tap your MagicBand or Key to the World Card within the specified time-frame on the light-up readers at the Lightning Lane entrances. Keep any cards out, as you may need to tap again.

You can only book Lightning Lane selections, one at a time. You'll need to redeem your current selection before booking the next one. However, if your next return time is more than two hours away, you'll be able to make another Lightning Lane selection, once a two hour cooling off period has passed. This way, if the only available return time for the attraction you wanted is in the evening, you'll still be able to book other return times during the day. Just note: the two hour cooling off period only applies to hours of operation. So if you booked a Lightning Lane selection at 7:00am, the two hour cooling off period won't start counting down until that particular park opens.

Whilst it's all pretty confusing to understand ahead of time, it's easier in practice.

Pro Tips for Disney Genie+

★ **Set reminders/alarms** - If you find yourself having to wait the two hour cooling off period before booking your next Lightning Lane selection, try to set an alarm. The app will not notify you when you can next book.

★ **If you're late** - Should you be running late to your return time, don't panic. Disney gives you a 15 minute grace period. Any time after that, it's up to the cast member's discretion and the circumstances.

★ **Refresh, refresh, refresh** - Disney Genie+ is a live system displaying the next available Lightning Lane return time. If someone cancels their return time, it goes back into the system. With that in mind, if the time you were hoping for isn't available, refresh the Tip Board a few times to see if a better time opens up. I find this process works best when targeting a particular attraction.

★ **Stacking** - Using the previously mentioned two hour rule, you can occasionally accrue three or four Lightning Lane return times all in quick succession of each other. This takes some practice and you'll only be able to do this for return times later in the afternoon/evening. But essentially, just keep booking selections every time your two hour cooling off period elapses, and by choosing return times around the same time later in the day.

★ **Use 7:00am** - The second it ticks over to 7:00am is when there's the best availability for popular attractions. On busy days, return times can go in seconds, so it pays to be one of the first guests on the Tip Board. If you miss out, fear not. Lots of people will be changing plans around this time, so keep refreshing for a few minutes and you may just snag what you wanted.

Is Disney Genie+ worth the money?

In my opinion, it depends on both your preferences, your budget, which park you're going to and how busy it is when you're visiting.

If you're planning a once-in-a-lifetime holiday and you'd like to reduce your time spent standing in line (as and when you can), then adding Genie+ to the length of your ticket is a nice upgrade to an already expensive holiday. "In for a penny, in for a pound" as they say. Some days you'll use it a lot, other days not at all. However, the hope is that over the course of your whole holiday, it gave you flexibility, saved you waiting in lines and evened out to be worth the cost.

If however you've got a budget to stick to, the length of ticket upgrade might not be right for you. Let's say you're paying about £500 per person for 14 day tickets; is an extra £100 per person worth it for the occasional Lightning Lane use? I personally don't think so. Not when you consider that could be a day at Universal, a few nice dinners, merchandise, you name it.

That being said, is it worth occasional use? Pay-as-you-go, if you will? Ultimately, the service is only as good as the availability on the day. If it's a reasonably quiet day/period (wait times averaging 45 minutes or less) and you're going to Magic Kingdom where lots of attractions have Lightning Lanes, then it's likely a good option. You'll likely save 30-40 minutes per attraction and have lots of availability throughout the day, as fewer guests feel the need to purchase Disney Genie+.

On a busy day and at somewhere like Animal Kingdom (with fewer attractions), I would avoid it like the plague. Through the sheer number of people using Genie+ and battling it out for the same return times, you may only get one or two Lightning Lane return times all day. Not great value for $15 per person.

All-in-all, Disney Genie+ is an expense. It depends on your personal circumstances as to whether that expense is worth it for the length of stay, for a couple of days or not at all. If you're unsure, my advice is to not add it on for length of stay and just see how you get on. Try it one day toward the start of your trip, and see how much use you get out of it and whether you feel like it was good value.

Which attractions come under Individual Attraction Selections?

This can vary, but as a rule of thumb, it's typically the top one or two most popular attractions in each park. For Hollywood Studios, this is currently Star Wars: Rise of the Resistance. Access to these attractions' Lightning Lanes, are not included in the Disney Genie+ service.

How much do Individual Attraction Selections cost?

The cost varies by attraction and season. The price for the attraction you're wishing to purchase Lightning Lane access for, will be displayed as a button below the estimated wait time on the app Tip Board.

On a busy day and for the most popular attraction in the park, you may be looking at $15 (+tax) per person. On a quiet day and a less popular attraction, this could be down to $7 per person. Unfortunately, there's no real way of knowing in advance.

How do you book Individual Attraction Selections?

From 7:00am, Disney resort guests will be able to book Individual Attraction Selections via the Tip Board. Guests staying off-property will be able to book once the park has opened.

On the Tip Board, the next available Lightning Lane return time will be displayed, as well as the current price per person. By tapping on this button, you will be able to select the people in your party that you'd like to purchase an Individual Attractions Selection for, as well as a preferred return time from what's available (which is different to Genie+). You will then need to complete the checkout process and pay for your Individual Attraction Selection within 10 minutes.

Are Individual Attraction Selections worth the money?

I would say, for some attractions yes and for others no. If the attraction is an absolute must for your holiday and the wait time will take away from your day, then the one-time cost may be a necessary evil in improving your day ten fold. With other attractions, for the sake of a 90 second "weeee," is $48 for a family of four really worth it on Seven Dwarfs Mine Train with a wait time of 45 minutes? I'm not so sure.

I would just consider the value for money, your budgeted spending money and how you're feeling on the day. How long is the wait? How long is the ride? How expensive is it going to be for us? Only you can decide what's reasonable to you.

Tips for Individual Attraction Selections

★ **Separate Service** - You don't have to buy Disney Genie+ to buy Individual Attraction Selections. These can be purchased as and when.

★ **Availability** - It's not uncommon for the most popular attraction to sell out. Your best bet is to be on the Tip Board at 7:00am if you're planning on buying one of these selections. You'll also have more choice of return times.

★ **Refunds and Cancellations** - It's important to note that these are non-refundable. If you change your plans and no longer wish to use your Individual Attraction Selection, you will forfeit the cost. However, in events where the ride breaks-down for example and does not resume operation that day, there may be exceptions made if you speak to Guest Relations before leaving.

★ **7:10am** - If you're up bright and early and miss out on the ideal return time, fear not. Since the system gives people 10 minutes to complete their transaction, normally after a few minutes (once people have seen the final price and decided against it), more return times will come back into the system. Just keep refreshing the Tip Board for a few minutes.

★ **Two Per Day** - It's worth noting you may only purchase two Individual Attraction Selections per person, per day. For example, you couldn't buy Lightning Lane return times for the two most popular rides in Hollywood Studios, ride those, park hop to Epcot and then do the same thing over there.

AIRPORT TRANSFERS

Unless you're planning on renting a car, you'll need to book transportation from Orlando International Airport (MCO), to your accommodation. Whilst ride share services like *Uber* and *Lyft* are available at MCO, the surcharge pricing is pretty painful and I'd recommend considering alternative transportation.

Mears Connect

If you're staying in Disney, my best recommendation would be Mears Connect. It's convenient, affordable, the drivers are friendly and they dispatch coaches regularly to the various Disney resorts. Overall, a good service in my opinion.

Change: Mears Connect is the most comparable service to the now discontinued Disney's Magical Express service.

Whilst Mears Connect offers both a Standard and Express service, the standard service is what most families will find suitable. This is a coach service to Disney that may make two or three stops along the way. From checking in to arriving at your hotel, I'd recommend allowing 40-75 minutes. The Express service is still a shared vehicle, it just takes fewer guests, should dispatch quicker and will go directly to your resort. It is however eye-wateringly expensive for what it is.

You can book Mears Connect on their website (*mearsconnect.com*) or at the coach terminal check-in desk.

Standard Pricing:

One Way: $16.00 per adult, $13.50 per child.
Return Service: $32.00 per adult, $27.00 per child.

Express Pricing:
Round Trip: $250 for up to 4 passengers, +$55 for each additional passenger.

Mears Connect Standard Service

If you book online, approximately 24 hours prior to your scheduled arrival at MCO, Mears will email you a QR code to scan at the coach terminal check-in. This is located on Level 1 of Terminal B (currently the same location as the former Disney's Magical Express service). You just walk all the way down, past the car rental desks to the end of Level 1.

At the check-in desk, you can either use one of the self-service tablets, or speak with a member of staff. Once checked-in, you'll be directed to join a line and await boarding of your coach. Various resort hotels will then be assigned to a coach. You'll leave your luggage with the driver to be packed onto the coach and then board.

The coach may wait 20-30 minutes for other passengers, but once departing the airport, the journey to Walt Disney World should only take 30-40 minutes.

Private Transfers

If there's 5 or more of you, it may be worth booking a private transfer. This should work out cheaper than Mears Connect and offer a private and direct service. Check reviews online if you're going with an independent transfer company.

BOOKING

Option 1: Do It Yourself

If you're booking 10 months or less in advance and you're happy to do some leg work, I strongly recommend the DIY system. The following steps will walk you through how to best book a trip in parts and for the best price.

Step 1 - Don't Choose Your Dates

Hopefully you'll have an idea of when you'd like to go but whatever you do, try not to settle on specific departure and return dates before you've even started looking at prices. The key to this process is getting you the cheapest flights possible and flight prices vary day-by-day. If you're able to be flexible with your dates, you may find yourself getting the deal of all deals!

Step 2 - Find Your Flights

I recommend using a flight comparison site like *skyscanner.net* to search flight prices for a particular month and then compare the different airlines. You can save soooooo much this way! Once you've had a look and narrowed down some dates, keep checking the prices for a week every day. I say this because flight prices change day-by-day. If it looks like a steal and you can afford it, BOOK IT!

Step 3 - Check Hotels

Once you've either decided on your flights or booked them, it's time to start looking at hotels. Whether you're staying on or off property, start by using a hotel comparison site to have a good look at what's available. At this stage, it doesn't matter which hotel you've decided on. This will allow you to see all prices for all hotels in the near-by area. A great hotel deal could change all the plans you had.

By using the map tool on sites like *Hotelscombined*, *Trivago* etc. you can quickly browse in Disney and near Disney. Don't just book the cheapest, make a shortlist and research each one.

Step 4 - Book Your Hotel

Once you've chosen a hotel (Disney or non-Disney), get quotes from the hotel's website, a travel agent/tour operator, or the hotel's call center and consider the comparison site price. That way you'll get a feel for which booking method is right for you and which is the best price/service/value for money.

When it's a Disney hotel, I will typically book direct with Disney or a tour operator (who will book direct for me). Whilst you may be able to save a little here and there, the price is normally comparable to third-party agents. The benefit with booking direct, is you get information straight from the horses mouth, Disney's customer service is excellent, you get all the Disney themed welcome packs/emails and you'll receive your ticket confirmations quicker.

Step 5 - Dining Plan

If you choose to stay in Disney and would like to book a dining plan, know you'll need to book your hotel, park tickets and dining plan all together. For more information on what the dining plan is, how it works and whether it's right for you, go back to page 69.

Step 6 - Park Tickets

This should be the last big ticket item (see what I did there). I'm sorry to say tickets will never be cheap. With on-the-day tickets in excess of $120 per person, per day - it's important to book your tickets in advance and with certified sellers. Personally, I book tickets through the official websites. If you're in the UK, I promise you, tickets are the cheapest before departure (e.g. Disney's 14 Day Ticket). Not only do they include the Memory Maker photo package, they're heavily discounted! *More info on tickets on page 74.*

Step 7 - Collate

With possibly everything booked in different places, it's important to print and collate all your booking confirmations in one folder.

Option 2: Package Holidays

If you're booking more than 10 months in advance, this will likely work best for you. When you want the booking process to be as care free as your actual holiday, a package deal can be the best way to achieve this. It's also what I'd recommend if you're set on having a rental car or flights aren't available yet.

Step 1 - Research

Even if you're set on a package deal, I recommend checking out the DIY method to booking (even if you just jot down an average cost of how much it'd cost to book everything separately). Going into booking your package with an idea of price, means you won't be taken for a mug when reviewing available packages.

Step 2 - Shortlist Some Package Holiday Companies

When it comes to package holiday providers, they're all very similar. If you're from the UK: Virgin Holidays, Tui, Ever After Holidays etc. are all selling the same Disney hotels, similar flights and similar rental cars. For that reason, open up a few website tabs, do your research and shortlist a few providers. Whilst all of them will be selling the same/similar products, it's going to come down to the service you receive, the holiday protection included and also the final price.

Step 3 - Check the Season

If you've already ran through the DIY process, you can go ahead and skip this step as you'll already have an idea of the cheapest arrival and departure dates.

Head to a flight comparison site like *skyscanner.net* and check flight prices for the time of year you're looking at travelling (if flights aren't on sale yet, have a look at the same month in an earlier year). You'll be able to see if there's a particular date when prices go through the roof. This is particularly important when booking a package over or near school holidays.

Step 4 - Shop Till You Drop

Now it's time to make some phone calls. Whilst website prices are a good indicator, you'll only ever get the best price from an agent over the phone. Make your way through your shortlist and get quotes for the same dates, hotel and flights from the different travel companies. You'll then have an idea on who you'd like to book with.

Step 5 - Book it!

Prices are only temporary. Once you've got a good price with an agent/company you like, book it as soon as possible.

Chapter 5
KNOW BEFORE YOU GO

Walt Disney World is approximately twice the size of Manhattan island. Even after living there for two years, I still haven't seen and done it all! Whilst you won't be able to do everything in one holiday, I think it's good to know the basics before you arrive. In this chapter I've given you all the pieces of information I think are good for any visitor to know, prior to arriving in Disney.

1. You will not be able to do everything.

I repeat! You will not be able to do everything! The only thing you'll get from trying to do everything is sore feet and a grumpy family. Know that it's just not possible and you should instead try to treasure and really experience the rides, shops and restaurants you do get to see.

2. Getting from place to place takes time.

In Walt Disney World, getting about can take anywhere from 15 - 90 minutes. Disney transport is great but when busy times hit, it may take far longer than you expected to get from point 'A' to point 'B'. If you've got a dining reservation to make, I recommend giving yourself at least an hour to get there.

3. Disney Buses

Bus transportation from your Disney resort hotel to the parks and Disney Springs is all complimentary. There should be a bus every 20-30 minutes, but they can sometimes be full from previous stops. In this case, they won't stop. It's also good to know that you may only board through the front door (for safety reasons). Buses begin running 45 minutes prior to park opening, and conclude service after the last guest has left the park.

4. There's more than burgers and chips.

A common misconception about Disney parks is that you'll be eating chicken nuggets, burgers and fries the entire time. Whilst you can certainly find these, every theme park and resort offers speciality food. In Epcot for example, you can literally eat your way around the world.

5. Adults can easily have a date-night.

Walt Disney World is not just for little ones. With outstanding fine-dining, bars and lounges, there's lots of opportunities for a magical date-night. With that in mind, select resort hotels have day-care and evening-care services to help the parents get a night to themselves. Even if you're not staying at Disney, these services are open to all guests (for a fee).

FUN FACT

Walt Disney World has more that 350 buses. Making it the third largest bus fleet in the state of Florida.

6. Construction is always happening.

Walt Disney World is the number one tourist destination in the world. It doesn't stay that way by staying the same. No matter when you go, you will most-definitely come across a couple of attractions under refurbishment, new attractions being built and/or some routine maintenance.

7. It will be busy.

Whilst you may have visited a local theme park on a day when every ride was a walk-on, those days are few and far between in Walt Disney World. No matter when you go, you're likely to experience some busy days in the parks. Use unofficial crowd forecasts to plan which parks are likely best for each day.

8. Wi-Fi

Whilst within the theme parks, hotels and Disney Springs, you'll have access to Disney's FREE guest wi-fi.

This is great for instant messaging, using the My Disney Experience app and general web browsing. It can be patchy at times however and isn't the fastest. For example, I wouldn't rely on it for streaming *Netflix* in your hotel room.

9. Don't be afraid to get lost.

Hopefully by now you've realised that Walt Disney World is big. It's only natural to get lost, especially if you've never been before. However, the cast members at Disney are never far away and will always be able to point you in the right direction (even if it's just finding the nearest restroom).

10. Be camera courteous.

You'll of course want to take pictures and videos during your trip. Whilst doing so, don't forget about the people around you. Try not to bring an iPad to film the fireworks and know ahead of time that selfie-sticks are banned in all Disney parks. It's also courteous to turn your flash off on rides, for fireworks and for shows.

11. Lovebug Season

For about four weeks around May and four weeks around September/October, you may find there's lots of little flying black bugs in the air. These are called Lovebugs, and whilst they're perfectly harmless, they are incredibly annoying. If you have a phobia of bugs or a little one that may be distressed by bugs landing on them, I might suggest visiting in other seasons or avoiding animal kingdom.

12. Tipping means something.

If you're from the UK, you're likely used to tipping only when service is beyond exceptional, safe in the knowledge staff are being paid a fair wage. In America, tipping isn't just a gesture, it's a custom. Servers in Walt Disney World for example get paid about $5 an hour (£3.50ish).

Tipping will always be at your discretion. However, I feel it's worth me explaining the tipping culture if you're not already familiar.

Some cast members won't make enough to support their family if a number of guests choose not to tip them that day. Coming from the UK, I appreciate the feeling of being confused by the American culture around tipping. However, it is what it is and having been on the other side of the equation, I know how much particular cast members rely on tips to live and what it means for someone to not tip when they've been provided a service.

A GUIDE TO TIPPING

Large Dining Parties - If you're a party of 6 or more, an 18% gratuity will be added to your bill. Servers normally have 3 or 4 tables. So this policy considers that if the server has a large party taking up most of their section for a hour or two, they cannot be left short for the service they have provided.

Servers and Bar Staff - Cast members in these roles are paid less than others. This is with the consideration that their role is 'tipped.' If buying a drink at a bar, it's customary to tip $1-2 per prepared drink. If you're dining at a table service restaurant where you're served by a cast member, consider the below percentages for working out how much to tip. If your server is terrible, of course you shouldn't tip them. However, I recommend speaking with a manger to explain why the service was terrible and why you won't be tipping.

JUST OK	GOOD	GREAT
15%	18%	20%+

Ride Share Services - Should you treat yourself to an Uber, Lyft or Minnie Van ride during your stay, you have the option of tipping in cash or via the app. Depending on the length of journey and the driver, I'd typically tip $3-10.

Bell Services - If you choose to have bell services store your bags, pick them up from your room or drop them off, I recommend tipping the host or hostess that assists you $1-2 per item of luggage. If I'm leaving my case with bell services on my last day for example, I'll typically tip when I pick them up.

Mears Connect - If you choose to use Mears' airport transfer service, consider tipping the driver at the end of your journey. Personally I opt for $2-3 per person, per journey. I'll normally have this in my hand prior to disembarking the coach and gift it to the driver when they offload my luggage.

Housekeeping - It's unlikely you'll have the same housekeeper for every day of your holiday. With that, I'd recommend leaving a tip each day, rather than a large tip at the end of your stay. I tend to tip $1-3 per person using the room, per day of service. I've also noticed that the housekeepers I've left tips for, have at times gone a little further to make my room even more magical. Should a housekeeper deliver extra pillows or something to the room, I'll normally tip them too.

Valet - If you choose to leave your car with the valet at the front of your Disney resort hotel (or at Disney Springs), I believe it's customary to tip when you drop off your car and when you pick it up. I don't have a real experience using this service but if the cast member assisting you has to run in the rain, consider tipping them more than just a couple of dollars.

Un-Tipped Cast Members - Not all cast members are allowed to accept tips. On occasion, a particular cast member may go above and beyond the call of duty. In this instance you may like to tip them as a way of thanks. However, don't be offended if they ask you to keep it. If a cast member is paid a certain hourly rate, they're not allowed to accept tips. However, a cast compliment can be a great way of thanking this cast member (page 115).

13. Disney Skyliner

This cabled gondola system provides quick transportation between: Epcot, Hollywood Studios, Disney's Riviera, Disney's Caribbean Beach, Disney's Art of Animation and Disney's Pop Century.

Each cabin can hold up to 10 guests. Guests will board as the gondola moves slowly through the station before it picks up speed when mounting the cable system. Regular service begins approximately 45 minutes prior to park opening and concludes about an hour after park closing.

Transferring

Caribbean Beach is the main station for the Skyliner. Within this hub, there are three lines that terminate. Here is where you will transfer to get to various destinations.

Delays and Stops

On occasion, the cable will slow or stop. This is perfectly normal and is to allow for cast members to assist a guest with any trouble boarding/disembarking their gondola. This is more typical on the Epcot line as Riviera doesn't have a dedicated special assistance station.

Emergency Procedure

In the event of a personal emergency, call boxes are located within each cabin. Should the system shut down, local authorities are trained to assist in a full system evacuation. Additionally, an emergency kit is located in each cabin which can be opened upon authorisation from a cast member.

Scared of Heights?

From someone who's scared of heights and claustrophobic, I'm pleased to say I love the Skyliner. It's a smooth journey, is beautifully quiet and can actually be very relaxing. If you're nervous and would like to 'try it out', I recommend travelling from Caribbean Beach to Pop Century/Art of Animation first.

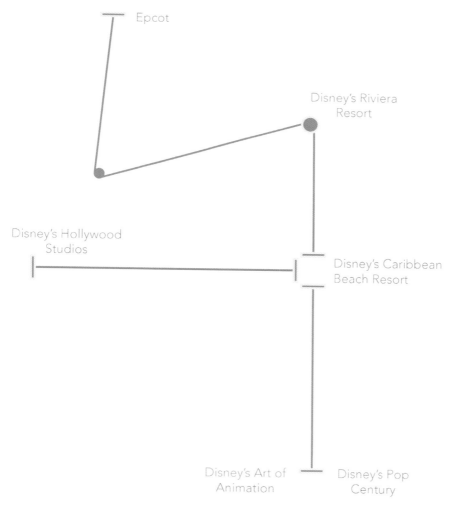

14. It's going to rain... A lot.

It storms a lot in Florida, to the extent that Florida is the world's capital for lightening strikes. No matter the time of year you're going, you're most likely going to get a few hours of rain. The only time of year you could potentially go an entire holiday without rain is December - March.

PRO TIP

If rain is forecast, consider taking some flip-flops with you. Change into them when it starts raining and keep your trainers nice and dry in your bag.

If you're travelling in Summer, expect it to rain every day between 3 - 5pm. Here's a couple of handy tips for managing the rain:

⭐ **Download a Weather Radar App** - The essential app for your time in Florida. Within 20 minutes, a storm can blow into your location. Most weather information is somewhat helpful but a radar will let you see what's heading your way in real-time.

⭐ **Store your Rain Gear** - If you're travelling with a few people, you don't want to be carrying lots of ponchos, flip flops and umbrellas all day. For that reason, consider renting a locker located at the main entrance of each park. Just keep an eye on your weather apps and when there's a storm coming, send one person to go grab the waterproofs. Locker rentals start at $10 per day for a small locker, which can perfectly hold four rain coats or so.

★ **Prepare for Closures** - If lightning comes within a particular radius of the parks, most outdoor attractions, merchandise and food locations are required to close for safety reasons. During the times where storms are most likely, get in line for indoor attractions or see if there's an indoor show coming up. Most guests panic when the rain starts, so it pays to plan ahead.

★ **Bide Your Time** - The first thing that happens when the heavens open is people leave the park. If you've come prepared for the rain, you'll find the park considerably quieter during and after the rain. Not to mention, all those outdoor attractions that have been closed will re-open with no lines! Big Thunder Mountain is a classic example of this. When the rain stops, head to these types of attractions. Just note it takes them about 30 minutes to get the all clear and for the attraction to get up and running again.

15. Alcohol

The minimum drinking age in the state of Florida is 21 years old. If you're from the UK and travelling with those between 18-21 years old, it can be frustrating. However, the drinking age in Florida is strictly enforced and this is something Disney takes very seriously.

If you're planning on handing off drinks to anyone underage or even trying to buy drinks underage, be prepared to not only get kicked out of the parks but to potentially be arrested.

Acceptable forms of I.D. are a U.S. issued driving license, a Passport or an international government issued I.D. WITH a copy or digital photograph of a passport. So if you're from the UK, just your driving license won't get you served. Either take a photo of your passport on your phone or have a photocopy with you to show alongside your UK driving license.

16. Photopass

Ever had a holiday where one person is always left out of the photo? Disney Photopass photographers are on hand in each park to capture some family memories. Whilst I wouldn't rely on these being the best photos of your trip, they're a nice way to get some group photos in popular spots.

⭐ **Memory Maker** - This is like a dining plan for photos. If not included in your park ticket, you can choose to buy this service ahead of your stay (currently $169 if bought at least 3 days in advance) or when you arrive (currently $199). This allows you to download as many digital photos from your stay as you like. Meaning you'll be able to get all your photos from rides, character meet & greets and photographers around the parks (e.g. photographers stationed in front of Cinderella's castle).

⭐ **Magic Shots** - With most Photopass photographers, you'll be able to get 'magic shots'. These place Disney characters in the photo with you or maybe have you floating away with a bunch of balloons. Just ask your Photopass photographer if they have magic shots available (not all of them do).

⭐ **Zoom Shots** - A Zoom Shot captures both a wide shot of the landscape and a close-up of your party. It then stitches these photos together to offer you a fantastic video memory. These services currently only operate when it's dry/ sunny. Ask a Photopass photographer for the closest Zoom Shot.

⭐ **On-ride Photos** - A lot of attractions have on-ride photos. However, they won't always be displayed at the ride exit. Some rides will add photos to your MDE account, by automatically detecting your MagicBand or Key to the World card. If you're missing an on-ride photo, stop-by one of the park's Photopass locations about 24 hours after the photo was taken.

17. Boarding Groups

With some of the popular attractions during peak seasons or when a new ride opens, you may need to get a Boarding Group in order to wait in line. Boarding Groups are typically released at 7:00am and can be booked via the MDE app. When your Boarding Group is called, you'll then be able to join the stand-by line. Boarding Groups are free but they can sell out, so act fast.

18. Guests with Disabilities

Disney do an amazing job of catering for all guests, no matter who they are or what their disability may be. Disney has a range of services that allow all guests to have an equal or as similar as possible experience. Whilst I suggest calling or visiting guest services to discuss individual needs, here's what I know:

★ **DAS Pass** - Disney provides a service known as Disability Access Service. This enables guests with a disability (including non-apparent) to use an adjusted waiting system when a disability may not allow you to wait in a standing line.

★ **Mobility** - If a guest's disability effects their mobility (e.g. they're required to use a wheelchair most of the time), the majority of lines for attractions are fully accessible (or they offer alternative lines when necessary).

★ **Sight/Hearing** - If a guest is hard of hearing or visually impaired, guests may obtain a handheld device that can offer assistance such as closed captioning and assistive listening. Devices can be obtained at guest services.

★ **Quiet Spaces** - Sometimes the parks get a bit 'much.' Check out the quiet spaces section for each park, later on in the guide.

19. Allergies

If someone in your party suffers from food allergies, it can be a constant worry that it's going to be difficult eating in restaurants. If you're a parent travelling with a little one with severe allergies, you're likely used to being in control. However, I'm here to assure you, you'll have plenty of options.

Disney has a well established allergy practice at all quick service and table service dining locations. The most important thing however, is for you to **let the first cast member you interact with know, that you have an allergy in your party**. This will in most cases be the restaurant greeter.

For most allergies, it'll be as simple as ordering from an allergy menu. These cater for common allergies such as dairy, eggs, gluten, peanuts etc. It's your responsibility to read this menu and order from it responsibly. You can however ask to speak with a chef if you have any questions.

If an allergy is not listed on these menus or is of high risk, let your server know what allergy you have and that you'd like to speak to a chef. Your server will give the chef a heads-up as to what your allergy is, allowing them to consult any recipes before speaking with you (and helping you order quicker). If requesting to see a chef, try to be patient as they're one of the busiest cast members in each location.

Chefs are specially trained to handle allergies with special attention and will, in most cases, have seen it all before. Don't be afraid to ask to speak to a chef whenever you have any questions or doubts. Disney takes safety incredibly seriously and is why they have strict allergy processes in-place to keep all guests safe.

20. Strollers (Prams / Push Chairs)

Little one's will often need strollers when at Disney, just because of how much walking they'll be doing. Even kids that haven't used a stroller for a while, may need one at Disney. Here's a couple of tips and tricks I've learnt from my days amongst strollers.

⭐ **Stroller Parking** - For safety reasons, strollers cannot be taken into certain spaces. These include attractions, shows, dining locations or certain pavilions within the parks. It's with this you'll need to park your stroller in a designated area outside the venue. Ask a cast member for the best location.

⭐ **Bring a Cover** - As your stroller will be outside in stroller parking, it's important to bring a cover to keep it dry in the event of a storm.

⭐ **Size Restrictions** - Some people like a stroller that can hold their child, their bag, their merchandise and the kitchen sink. However, guests should note that Disney has size restrictions for strollers. A stroller can be no larger than 31 inches wide and 52 inches long.

⭐ **Disney Transport** - For some methods of Disney Transport, you'll be required to fold your stroller before boarding. This is where a smaller stroller comes in very handy.

21. Stroller/ Wheelchair Rentals

Sometimes the unexpected happens. Someone twists their ankle or a child you never expected to whine about walking, just gives up. You can rent strollers and wheelchairs at the entrance of each park. Rentals are currently priced at $15 for a single child stroller, $31 for a double child stroller, $12 for a wheelchair and $70 for an electric scooter/ECV ($20 refundable deposit) per day. Keep ahold of your receipt if you park hop, as the fee covers all day and all parks. Rentals are available on a first come, first served basis and can occasionally sell out.

22. Meeting Characters

Characters are a huge part of the Disney experience. The best way to find where characters are going to be is on the My Disney Experience app. Here you'll find a handy symbol that labels character locations and times they'll be appearing.

For most characters you'll need to line-up. However, a number of them offer Disney Genie+ return times and Disability Access Service. Some characters have designated times (like Snow White in Epcot) and their line will be closed when it's coming towards the end of their set. Others will be continuous, but don't be alarmed if Pluto leaves to get a bowl of water. He'll be right back.

All characters will be with an attendant. They are there to manage the line and look after the character throughout their set. They'll often be happy to take pictures for you when a photographer isn't around.

When meeting the characters, try to keep the magic alive for the little ones around you. Ask Cinderella about her Fairy Godmother, tell Daisy she's looking fabulous or let Donald know you think he's number one. Some people (I'm not saying you) may choose to test the magic with what they say to characters or ask cast members. Magic is real, especially in Disney. Let's just leave it at that.

Tips for Meeting Characters

⭐ **Be Courteous to Other Guests** - If you're in line and someone ahead of you is currently with a character, don't rush them. This may be the only character they've wanted to meet all holiday. Likewise, if you like to chat with the characters, by all means do; just keep other guests in mind with how long you choose to talk to them.

⭐ **Photographers** - Some photographers will get involved, suggesting poses and taking a couple of snaps. However, if you want another picture or specific pose, just ask. Not all photographers take the best photos...

⭐ **Autographs** - Whilst most characters are more than happy to sign autograph books, some may not have opposable thumbs to be able to do so (e.g. Baymax and Olaf). To help characters, I recommend getting clickable sharpies and to open your autograph book to the next blank page.

⭐ **Bags** - When you're next in line, remove your bags. When you go to meet the character, place these down toward the exit to help the cast members.

23. Show Times

Disney has some of the best shows in the theme park industry. So much so, you won't want to miss them! My advice is to check the Times Guide (either on paper or in the My Disney Experience app) and arrive about 30 minutes before show time. This is to ensure you get a good view.

Due to limited capacity, some shows may fill up before the show's even close to starting. My advice is to stop-by ahead of the show you'd like to catch and ask a cast member how far in advance they recommend you arrive.

24. Parade & Fireworks

When it comes to one time performances like the parade and fireworks, don't be afraid to get a spot about 45 minutes before the show. Especially with the parade, if you want a spot in the shade, expect to wait for it. This is the process I'd recommend for your first time watching any given performance.

Once you've seen something once, you've then got the opportunity to rock-up last minute and take your chances. When it comes to fireworks in Epcot, don't worry too much about getting a spot directly on the lagoon. The World Showcase promenade is so wide, that even back from the lagoon-side you'll have a great view of the fireworks. The only time rocking-up last minute doesn't work, is during busy times with performances that have a limited capacity such as Fantasmic in Hollywood Studios.

25. Smoking Areas

Smoking and vaping is not permitted anywhere inside the theme parks. This is enforced by all cast members for the comfort and well-being of all guests. Designated smoking areas are located outside the theme parks and in select areas at the resorts and Disney Springs.

26. Height Requirements

Most rides at Disney have a height requirement. If a little one doesn't measure-up, know that there is no amount of bargaining or pleading that'll let them through. It's a restriction for a reason.

PRO TIP

Measure any little ones before departure and review the height requirements on Disney World's website to manage expectations.

27. Merchandise

You're bound to 'treat yourself' on your dream holiday. The following tips will help make your shopping time as magical as can be:

⭐ **See It, Get It** - If you see something you like, don't assume you'll be able to get it later on your trip. More often than you think, sought-after products will sell out and aren't always stocked elsewhere.

⭐ **Resort Delivery** - If you're staying in a Disney hotel, you can send merchandise back to your hotel's merchandise store. This will be available for collection after 4pm the next day. It's worth noting that this service cannot be used on your last full day, so plan ahead if you're buying heavy/bulky items.

⭐ **Package Pick-Up** - You can also send your merchandise to the front of the park for pick-up on the way out. However, the package pick-up point is very busy at the end of each day, so I wouldn't recommend this service if you're staying until park close.

⭐ **Virtual Locker** - If you find yourself purchasing a Lightsaber at Hollywood Studios, these don't exactly fit in the standard lockers. A virtual locker currently costs $10 and is a way to store bulky items. This is currently only available at the Hollywood Studios stroller/wheelchair rental store near the park entrance. Standard lockers are also available for storing smaller items.

⭐ **Returns** - Should you need to return an item, you can return all Disney Parks merchandise to any Disney merchandise store on property. However, be sure to keep your receipts.

28. Room Occupied Policy

Unlike other hotels, Disney has a room occupied policy. This policy means that whilst you're welcome to turn down housekeeping and use your hotel room for privacy, a Disney cast member is required to enter the room every 24 hours. This is for the improved safety of all guests.

29. Drinking Water

It's so important to stay hydrated during your stay in Florida. It's recommended to drink about eight pints of water a day (on average). With this, know that the Disney parks all provide regular water fountains and you can get a FREE cup of water from any quick service location. Bottled water is very expensive.

30. Entering the Parks

It's important to note that your park tickets should be linked to your My Disney Experience account. Without this, your MagicBand/Key to the World Cards will not act as your park ticket.

When you enter the parks for the first time, you'll be required to choose a finger that will be associated with your ticket. You will need to scan this finger each time you enter the parks. Children who's fingers may be too small to scan, may require an adult to use theirs. Make sure this is an adult that will always be entering the parks with them.

31. Attraction Refurbishments

During slower periods (typically Winter), Disney may close attractions for routine maintenance. They'll advertise these closures on their website, so you can know ahead of time whether any of your favourites may be unavailable.

32. Delivery to a Resort Hotel

If you're making a reasonable journey to Walt Disney World, you may want to order some groceries or online shopping to your hotel. It's important to know that the mailing address for resort hotels is different to that displayed on Google. For the correct address, call +1 407 W-DISNEY (+1 407-934-7639).

Add your arrival date to the name on the delivery and make sure you don't order anything more than a week before check-in. If your delivery arrives during your stay, it should be delivered to your hotel room during the day. All resort deliveries come with a small handling fee. It takes about 24 hours to go through Disney's sorting office, so count that into your order timings.

PRO TIP

At the start of your holiday, make a trip over to Premium Outlets on Vineland Avenue. There you'll find a magical little store called Disney's Character Warehouse. Within this store you'll find official discontinued and discounted Disney Parks merchandise. This is great for treating little ones to affordable souvenirs.

33. Annual Pass

If you think an annual pass is only right for people who will be visiting all the time, think again! A Walt Disney World annual pass allows you to get 20% off merchandise (excluding select limited edition merchandise), up to 20% off select dining locations, FREE parking and even discounts on hotel rooms. It may work out beneficial for just one person in your party to upgrade to an annual pass to get all of those benefits. This is likely the case if you're travelling with a big group and plan to spend most of your time in Disney.

Whilst there are four tiers to annual pass, as an international guest you'll only be able to get the top tier: Incredi-pass. If you've got the UK 14 day ticket, this can easily be upgraded into an annual pass for approximately $650 (£480ish). This works out about the same cost as getting another 14 day ticket. So, if you're planning on visiting within the next year, this could be a great way to pre-pay for admission on your next trip, whilst also using those discounts on both holidays. If you're planning on visiting more than twice in the next year, it's a no-brainer.

Should you wish to use your passholder discount on a resort stay, just note this is for a room only reservation (so you can't add the dining plan necessarily). Passholder discounts typically become available 3/4 months prior to travel and can only be booked through the stateside call center. To book, call:

+1 407 WDW-STAY
(+1 407 939-7829)

If you'd like to get through to an agent quickly, just keep pressing 0 at the various prompts.

34. Bringing in Your Own Food

You're welcome to bring food with you into the parks (as long as it's within reason). For safety reasons, cooler boxes and ice are not allowed into the parks. If looking to keep food cool, consider freezer blocks. Should you wish to bring snacks/lunch into the parks, make sure your food is stored in a transparent box so that you're not held up at security. I strongly advise against using tin foil to wrap your sandwiches, as this can spark alarm bells when going through security.

35. Cast Member Compliments

During your holiday, you may come across a cast member that goes above and beyond to make your trip magical. It's worth noting their name, work location and the time you encountered them. If you'd like this cast member to be recognised in some way, you can either:

★ Visit Guest Services at the entrance of each park or in Town Center at Disney Springs. Here you can send an Applause-o-gram which is a very special recognition. It's not every day a guest will go out of their way to write an Applause-o-gram and it's worth a lot of brownie points to the cast member.

★ Write a letter/email after your trip. This is often a useful method if a cast member truly made your holiday and you're reflecting on the stand-out moments from your trip.

36. Guest Experience Team

Throughout the parks, you may notice cast members dressed in blue under blue umbrellas. These are essentially field guest services cast members. Whilst they can't do everything, they're able to answer most questions, assist with My Disney Experience, amend Genie+ return times and more.

FUN FACT

Walt Disney World has it's own doggy day care and cattery on property.

37. Ride Share Services

Sometimes, Disney Transport just won't cut it. Whether the buses just aren't on your side, or you're thinking of venturing off property, services like Uber and Lyft come in very handy whilst visiting Orlando.

In my experience, a great use of a ride share service is going from your hotel, to another hotel. Typically for a dining reservation. The few dollars spent on your ride share, can save you taking a bus to one of the theme parks, to then take another bus to your destination hotel.

In my opinion, a poor use of a ride share is at Magic Kingdom. Since the ride share pick-up/drop-off location is a whole lagoon away at the Transportation and Ticket Center, you'll need to get a monorail or ferry boat from there to get to the park entrance. The bus station however, is right at the park entrance. So you'll almost always be better off waiting for the bus when going to Magic Kingdom.

If you're looking for express transport whilst remaining on Walt Disney World property, Disney do have a premium Minnie Van service. These can be booked through the Lyft app, and whilst pricey, can drop you right at the park entrances or even right outside your Disney hotel room.

38. Portable Phone Chargers

Since you'll be using your phone for everything from Mobile Order to Genie+, it's worth investing in a decent portable charger. You'll be shocked how quickly your phone battery depletes each day. I'd recommend finding a charger that can hold at least 2 or 3 full charges and has fast charging capability. Additionally, the lighter the better. No one wants to be carrying a brick around on holiday.

39. Footwear

Whilst you may want to wear that new shiny pair of shoes you bought for your holiday, whatever you do, break them in before your go.

It's so important to have comfortable and reliable shoes for the amount of walking you'll be doing in Disney. I would recommend a pair of proper running trainers.

40. Data Roaming

Before departing for the U.S., check what your phone provider's data roaming charges are. If the cost is too much, be sure to switch off data roaming in your settings prior to landing in Orlando. I've been guilty of forgetting about it and coming home to a frighteningly high phone bill.

41. Park Hopping

Should you wish to visit more than one park on the same day, you'll first need to visit the park you have a Park Pass for, then wait until park hopping begins in the afternoon. Currently this time is 2:00pm. UK tickets automatically include park hopping, but with other US tickets, this is an optional upgrade.

42. Sun Protection

Considering Florida is called the Sunshine State, it's incredibly important to consistently put on sun cream. I find myself using an SPF 50 designed for babies (you can buy it in the hotel merchandise store) and I'm not someone who burns easily. Whilst you may want to get a tan on holiday, I assure you, it's not worth the agony of putting your park bag on sunburnt shoulders. Trust me. I also highly recommend topping up throughout the day, even when it's cloudy.

43. Security

Security is a big deal in Disney. There are multiple types of security in use to help keep you safe and help you feel safe. These include security officers, bag checks and CCTV.

The security check at each park is pretty seamless, in that you pass through two pillars in a single file line without stopping. You don't need to remove your bags or take out metal items. The scanners can detect objects on your person that may be of concern. If you get beeped, you'll just be asked to have your bag checked by one of the security guards and/or potentially wanded. If you have a pushchair or wheelchair, you may be directed to an alternative line.

If you happen to have something that's metal and very dense in your bag (e.g. an umbrella, portable charger, camera batteries etc.), take it out of your bag and hold it out in front of you. As you walk through the scanners, if that item is the thing that gets beeped, you won't necessarily have to get your bag manually checked.

Disney is private property. As such, they maintain the right to eject any guest from the resort at any time. They're also not afraid to ban guests from their properties, should any behaviour warrant such a consequence. With that in mind, I recommend reviewing Disney's code of conduct online and ensuring everyone in your party adheres to these rules throughout the trip. Loosing your temper with a cast member or having one drink too many, isn't worth a lifetime ban from the most magical place on earth.

44. Emergencies

For minor injuries, visit First Aid within the parks or ask to see a first aider when outside of the parks. For major injuries or fire, call 911 and tell the operator you're in Walt Disney World and need Reedy Creek. They're Disney's on-site response team. Any other major emergencies, call 911.

45. Healthcare

In a worst case scenario, you may need urgent medical assistance. Advent Health is Walt Disney World's official healthcare partner. They have two urgent care facilities, one near Disney Springs and one near Animal Kingdom.

Providing you don't need an ambulance, Advent Health offer complimentary transportation from Walt Disney World property to their 24 hour, 7 days a week healthcare centers. You just need to call them on:

+1 407-939-2273

They will then give you an estimated time for pick-up. After your visit, they will also drop you back free of charge. What won't be free, is your actual appointment. All healthcare in the U.S. needs to be paid for. Whilst your travel insurance may be accepted, it's important to check the moment you walk through the door. The last thing you want is a medical bill in the thousands.

Advent Health is useful for things like:

★ Allergies
★ Cold & Flu Symptoms
★ Rashes & Sunburn
★ Injuries needing X-ray or stitches
★ And other non-emergency health issues.

Chapter 6
MAGIC KINGDOM

Opened in 1971, Magic Kingdom is the single most attended theme park in the world! Growing up, it was a place of legend and I'd have been so lucky to ever go. Now, I'm very lucky to know it like the back of my hand. I've got attraction recommendations, I can let you know where's good to eat and even share how to get a great position for the fireworks.

What I'm not going to do is waste your time here. You've got things to do and characters to see. I'm simply going to share my best tips, tricks and advice when it comes to spending a day at Magic Kingdom.

FUN FACT

Hidden inside the castle is Cinderella's Royal Suite. This is the room in Disney you can't book. Guests are either gifted a night's stay or win one.

TOP TIPS

Whilst I'm going to walk you through as much of the park as I can, there are some top line things everyone should know when visiting Magic Kingdom. These top tips are great if you're on the go and need a little reminder.

- ★ **Parking** - Magic Kingdom (and all the parks for that matter) require a parking fee. Currently this is $25 per car. When approaching the toll plaza, be ready to pay.

- ★ **Getting to the park** - The parking lot is HUGE. It'll take some time to walk or use the tram to reach the front of the lot. At the front of the lot is the Transportation and Ticket Center.

- ★ **Transportation and Ticket Center (TTC)** - This area is the middle ground between the parking lot and the actual theme park. Between the park and the parking lot is a lake. To get to the park you have to take a monorail or ferry from the TTC. It's in this area you'll go through security and be able to buy tickets (if you haven't already).

- ★ **Security** - Since Magic Kingdom is the biggest tourist destination in the world, security is tight. Be prepared to have your bags and strollers checked and go through walking scanners. This is necessary to ensure your safety in the park and give you peace of mind. The security team are always a welcoming face of the parks.

* **Welcome Show** - About 30 minutes before opening time, you'll be able to enter the park and make your way up to Cinderella's castle for the welcome show. When the park officially opens, Mickey and his pals will welcome you to Magic Kingdom with a mini stage show.

* **'Rope Drop'** - If you've done some research, you might have seen this term already. It's more literal than it seems. Cast members will block off each land of the Magic Kingdom prior to the official opening time with a rope. Once the park has been announced open, guests will be able to explore the rest of the kingdom. Getting to a park for 'rope drop' is just getting there for opening.

* **Postcards Home** - If you want to send a letter or postcard home, you can send it from Magic Kingdom and have a special stamp added to the envelope. Stamps are sold at the small shop located to the far left of the train station near the entrance.

* **You'll Need More Than One Day** - With so much to see and do at Magic Kingdom, it's unlikely you'll be able to see everything in just one day.

* **Rider Swap** - If you've got a little one that's too short for a ride, ask a cast member for a rider swap pass. Only one parent will have to line-up to ride. Once off, swap parenting and the other parent will use the Lightning Lane.

* **Shop During the Day** - Some may tell you that because the shops are open late, you should wait until the end of the day to do your shopping. However, the shops are a lot more enjoyable during the day. With delivery services to your hotel or the front of the park, you shouldn't need to carry anything.

Attractions

There are more attractions in Walt Disney World than you can shake a stick at. So whilst I'd love to give you a detailed description of each and every ride, I still want this book to be light enough to take with you on holiday. With that, I'm going to name each attraction, share my priority rating, who I think it's good for (typically speaking) and which weather it's best enjoyed in. If there's a ride you'd like more information on, check the My Disney Experience app or see if there's a video on YouTube that'll give you a point-of-view preview.

PRO TIP

If you've never been to Walt Disney World before, download the My Disney Experience app and browse the park maps as I'm walking you through the parks. You'll get a better idea of what I'm talking about when you see it in front of you.

Adventureland

Located to the left of Cinderella's castle when entering the park, Adventureland is where I recommend starting your day if you arrive for opening. Most people turn right when given the choice or head straight to Fantasyland.

Themed like a jungle and featuring the popular Jungle Cruise, you'll feel like you're really on an adventure in this area.

Jungle Cruise

Magic Carpets of Aladdin

Pirates of the Caribbean

Swiss Family Treehouse

Enchanted Tiki Room

FUN FACT

Pirates of the Caribbean was not an opening day attraction. It was only when guests shared their disappointment in it's absence, did they find a place to squeeze it in.

Frontierland

Saddle up partners, we're headed to the old frontier! With it's western style theming and some of the best attractions in the park, Frontierland is one of my favourite lands to hang out in. Another great land to head to when the park first opens!

PRO TIP

Frontierland is the start of the parade route. Whether you're looking to watch the daytime, Halloween or Christmas parade, it's a little quieter here.

Big Thunder Mountain

✦ ✦ ✦ ✦ ✦

It's a roller coaster but one that's all about the fun. Possibly my favourite ride in the park or at least my 'must-do.' Big Thunder Mountain is always quietest when the sun goes down and riding it in the dark offers a little extra thrill. This is a good first roller coaster for little ones.

Country Bear Jamboree

✦ ✦ ✦ ✦ ✦

Splash Mountain

✦ ✦ ✦ ✦ ✦

Tom Sawyer's Island

Liberty Square

Think colonial America around the time of the Revolutionary War. Here you can see a replica of the Liberty Bell, take a steam boat around Tom Sawyer's Island or venture into the infamous Haunted Mansion. I recommend Momento Mori for some ghostly shopping.

Haunted Mansion

FUN FACT

Throughout the Haunted Mansion, there are special pressure sensors. If a guest steps out of their Doom Buggy, these will immediately shut down the ride.

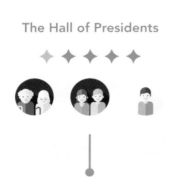

The Hall of Presidents

Liberty Square Riverboat

PRO TIP

If you're looking for a good place to watch the parade, consider just outside the Christmas Shop courtyard. Perfectly shaded and super close to the fun.

Fantasyland

Let your inner-child run free in this land of fantasy and make-believe. Featuring some of the most popular and most recognisable Disney attractions, you don't want to miss out on these. It's quietest here when the parade is on or during/after the fireworks.

Dumbo the Flying Elephant

Enchanted Tales with Belle

It's A Small World

Mad Tea Party

Mickey's PhilharMagic

Peter Pan's Flight

Prince Charming Regal Carrousel

Princess Fairytale Hall

Pete's Silly Sideshow

Seven Dwarfs Mine Train

The Barnstormer

The Many Adventures of Winnie The Pooh

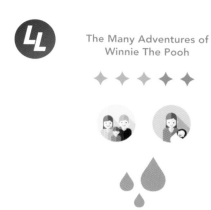

Under the Sea: Journey of The Little Mermaid

PRO TIP

Seen the fireworks before and don't want to wait around for a good spot? Consider watching them from the Tangled toilets in Fantasyland.

Tomorrowland

Step into the world of what could've been the future. Styled in a 50s-esque idea of what the future was going to look like, you'll find some of the hottest attractions here. I can easily spend an entire afternoon just hanging about in Tomorrowland.

Buzz Lightyear's Space Ranger Spin

Monsters Inc. Laugh Floor

Astro Orbiter

Space Mountain

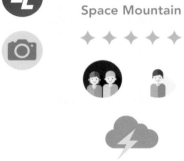

Space Mountain is one of those rides I will giggle like a school girl all the way round. Whilst most of the queue for this roller coaster is indoors, it's not a pleasant line to stand in. As such, a Lightning Lane return time may be worth the investment on this one.

Tomorrowland Speedway

PeopleMover

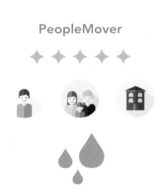

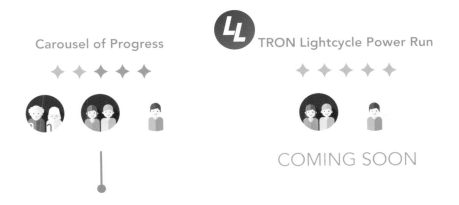

Carousel of Progress

✦ ✦ ✦ ✦ ✦

TRON Lightcycle Power Run

✦ ✦ ✦ ✦ ✦

COMING SOON

Dining

So, where does one eat in the most visited theme park on earth? Well, there's more than a few places to grab a snack or sit down for a feast. Having tried every quick service and table service in the park, I'll give you my top recommendations for each style of dining.

Quick Service Dining

The quick service restaurants at Magic Kingdom are busy most of the time. As such, I'd recommend them for families on-the-go.

If possible, try to dine outside of peak meal times for a more relaxing experience. I'd try to avoid: 12pm - 2pm and 5pm - 7pm.

Columbia Harbour House

By far my favourite dining location in Magic Kingdom, this quick service serves New England style home comforts such as Chicken Pot Pie, Lobster Roles and more. Head upstairs for ample seating and a nice chill away from the hustle and bustle of the park.

Be Our Guest

Available at breakfast and lunch, Be Our Guest's quick service is great for Beauty and the Beast fans! How often do you get the chance to dine in the Beast's ballroom? I wouldn't recommend going here for dinner, as compared to breakfast and lunch, it's overpriced and not great food.

Pecos Bill Tall Tale Inn & Cafe

If, like me, you enjoy Mexican food; you'll likely enjoy grabbing lunch here. With a great selection of what I call 'pick-me-up' food and free toppings, it's well worth your time and money. It can feel a little crowded at times so I wouldn't hang-out here too long.

Table Service Dining

If you're looking for the chance to kick-back, unwind and have a break from a busy day, these table service recommendations may be right for you. I've only included a couple here as there are better table service locations outside of the park.

Skipper Canteen

Whilst the menu may be a little 'out there' for some, the atmosphere and cast member interaction at this location is something truly special! You're served by a Jungle Cruise skipper and they're just as sarcastic and witty as they are on the Jungle Cruise attraction.

The Crystal Palace

If you're looking for a character breakfast, look no further. Whilst an expensive breakfast, this all-you-care-to-enjoy buffet features Winnie the Pooh and friends, as well as a great selection of food. Reservations are highly recommended for this restaurant.

Quiet Spaces

In Magic Kingdom especially, the parks can feel a little overwhelming. I myself really struggle with crowds. After standing in amongst a lot of people, I just need a little me time to relax before continuing with the day. The below spaces should give you some time to calm down and recuperate.

★ **Columbia Harbour House** - The upstairs of this Quick Service dining location (ideally outside of busy dining hours) is quiet and air conditioned.

★ **Tom Sawyer's Island** - As long as you don't mind a small boat ride over to the island, this is by far the best place to relax. With rocking chairs and plenty of shade, it's a great place to escape whilst still exploring.

★ **Tortuga Tavern** - This quick service is only open when demand requires it to be open. Outside of those times, it's a great place to chill.

★ **Hub Grass** - Whilst not that quiet, located in-front of Casey's Corner, you can just lay down on astroturf and soak up the sun if you so choose.

★ **Tangled Toilets** - Whilst I'm not suggesting you hang out in the toilets, there's some seating and covered space just across from the restroom building. Some of the benches also have outlets to charge your phone.

★ **Main Street** - There's a small side-street off Main Street by Uptown Jewlers. A nice quiet area with some tables and chairs. Handy when Main Street's a bit much or you're waiting for your family in the merchandise stores.

★ **First Aid** - Worst comes to worst, head to First Aid if you feel like you may be on the verge of a panic attack.

Entertainment

Magic Kingdom is entertainment central! With a parade, castle stage show, pop-up shows and more, you'll be spoilt for choice. As Magic Kingdom is targeted at families with young children, the majority of shows will gear more to this audience, but will bring a smile to any child at heart.

Mickey's Magical Friendship Faire

✦ ✦ ✦ ✦ ✦

Main Street Philharmonic

✦ ✦ ✦ ✦ ✦

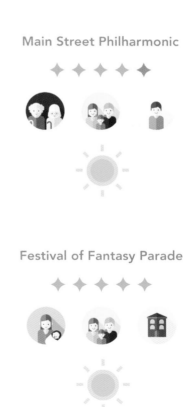

Dapper Dans

✦ ✦ ✦ ✦ ✦

Festival of Fantasy Parade

✦ ✦ ✦ ✦ ✦

Rainy Day Cavalcade

If you're lucky enough to be in Magic Kingdom when it's raining (stay with me) and it's not a thunder storm, the Festival of Fantasy parade turns into the Rainy Day Cavalcade. You need a lot of luck to see this parade. If you do, you'll get to see characters in cute rain coats.

Adventure Friends Cavalcade

Main Street Trolley Show

Enchantment (Fireworks)

Here's one for everyone! Enchantment is Magic Kingdom's nighttime firework spectacular. This show features projection mapping on the castle, fireworks, lasers and Tinkerbell may even fly through the night (weather permitting). A great way to end your evening on a high.

Merchandise

Everyone loves to treat themselves to a souvenir on holiday. Well, in Magic Kingdom you'll have a lot of choice to satisfy your inner shopaholic. Below are a few tips and tricks to snap up your keepsakes. Don't forget about package pick-up or delivery back to your Walt Disney World resort hotel.

⭐ **Main Street Emporium** - By far the largest store in the park, this merchandise location covers all the buildings on the left side of Main Street U.S.A. Whilst it's open about an hour after park closing, I recommend visiting this store about midday. After the parade and after the fireworks are by far the busiest times to shop in here.

⭐ **Memento Mori** - Located across from Columbia Harbour House is a merchandise store with a twist. This store is dedicated to The Haunted Mansion. Not only can you pick-up some spooky souvenirs, you can also get a haunting portrait done to make you one of the 999 happy haunts.

⭐ **Bonjour! Village Gifts** - Located next to Gaston's Tavern, this store sells popular Disney art and figurines.

PRO TIP

If you don't want to wait over an hour for the perfect fireworks view, arrive about 30 minutes before show-time. People sitting on the floor will be asked to stand, which opens-up space. Kindly ask people to excuse you as you make your way to the space at the back of the Walt and Mickey statue. Hasn't failed me yet!

Welcome to my home park!

Epcot is where I proudly represented the United Kingdom for two years within the Rose & Crown pub & restaurant. Having spent my mornings walking to work through the park and countless afternoons enjoying the park, I know Epcot better than anywhere else.

Opened in 1982, Epcot was the second park to be built in Walt Disney World. Derived from the words experimental, prototype, community of tomorrow; Epcot was originally designed by Walt to be a living and breathing city that had residents experimenting with different ways of living in the modern world.

Whilst Walt's original idea wasn't realised, the park is my personal favourite with state-of-the-art attractions and a showcase of cultures from around the world. Starting back in 2019, Epcot embarked on a new journey to reinvent the look of the park and introduce some new life to what had become a pretty dated aesthetic. As with most refurbishments, Disney will execute each part in phases. With this in mind, excuse the extra pixie dust over the coming years.

FUN FACT

Epcot's Spaceship Earth is adorned with 11,324 triangular tiles; the same number of spaces in the parking lot. The gaps in-between the tiles filter rain water into World Showcase lagoon.

TOP TIPS

If you're visiting Epcot, here's some top tips that will help you navigate your day. As it's a park with a completely different vibe to that of Magic Kingdom, it's best to keep the major differences in mind before visiting.

⭐ **Walking** - The route around World Showcase Lagoon is approximately 1.3 miles. It's all too easy to get caught up in the fun, walk 20,000+ steps and end up with sore feet. As such, I highly recommend wearing comfortable shoes and taking regular breaks throughout the day.

⭐ **Bring ID** - If you'd like to get an alcoholic drink, make sure you have the right ID (page 103).

⭐ **International Gateway** - Epcot has the advantage of two entrances. The main entrance is situated in front of Spaceship Earth (the golf ball) and the other is nestled in the back between the UK pavilion and the France pavilion. If you're staying at the Yacht & Beach Club, Boardwalk or Swan & Dolphin hotels, this will be your main entrance to the park. Likewise, this is where the Skyliner station is located for service from Rivera, Caribbean Beach, Art of Animation and Pop Century. At park closing, lines for the Skyliner can get very long. My advice is to hang-around or leave before the fireworks finish.

⭐ **Club Cool** - Located between the Creations Shop and Connections Cafe, this *Coca-Cola* merchandise store, allows you to try different sodas from around the world. This is a great place to cool down and enjoy everyone's reactions to some of the best and worst sodas you'll ever try.

★ **Harmonious** - Each evening, Epcot presents their nighttime spectacular in the middle of World Showcase Lagoon. Whilst the main circular screen faces the front of the park, you can get a great view from anywhere around the Lagoon. Some of my favourite spots include the UK pavilion, Germany, Japan and Mexico. Because of this, it isn't necessary to stake out a spot for ages.

★ **Rope Drop** - You'll want to be at park opening if you're looking to get on the most rides possible. As Epcot has a greater attendance past 12pm, those first few hours in the morning are your prime opportunity to ride like the wind!

★ **World Showcase** - This is the area of the park that features 11 pavilions from around the world. Each pavilion hosts dining and merchandise, with some also including films and attractions. Most of World Showcase doesn't open until 11am and tends to be quieter when it first opens.

★ **Lunch on the Showcase** - As I've mentioned above, World Showcase opens at 11am. If you don't have a lunch reservation, head to one of the Showcase restaurants just before 12pm as they're opening. You'll normally be able to score a walk-in reservation without much of a wait.

★ **Events** - Epcot is known for it's annual Food & Wine festival (especially amongst locals). However, this and other festivals make the world showcase uncomfortably busy sometimes. If visiting during an event, try and complete the Showcase before 4pm to avoid large crowds and long lines.

Attractions

One of the great things about Epcot is that almost every attraction is undercover. If you're forecast rain on your holiday, see if you can make it to Epcot for this day. When storms hit, there's very little in Epcot that has to close.

Epcot has some of my favourite attractions. Frozen Ever After is a must-do for any Frozen fan and Test Track will satisfy anyone with a need for speed.

World Celebration

As part of Epcot's transformation, the former Future World has been spilt into three different sections. I'll walk you through each new area, starting off in World Celebration. This is now the main spine of the park, encompassing the front entrance and the plaza leading up to World Showcase.

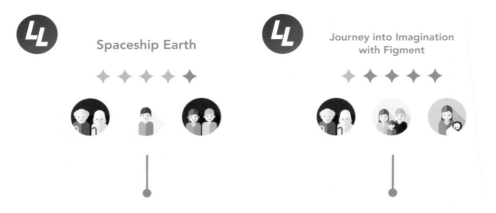

Spaceship Earth

Journey into Imagination with Figment

World Nature

Celebrating the wonders of our world, the attractions in World Nature focus on how we interact with the natural world. Here you can soar over the Great Wall of China, find yourself in the middle of a giant aquarium or even learn how Walt Disney World grow their own food.

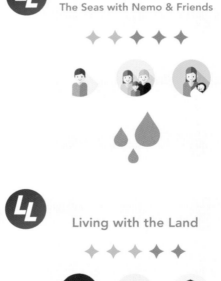

The Seas with Nemo & Friends

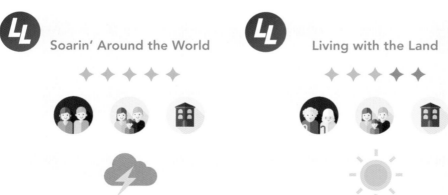

Soarin' Around the World

Living with the Land

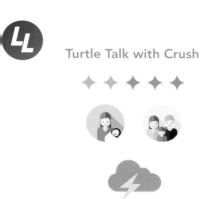

World Discovery

The home of innovative attractions and a step into the future. World Discovery is dedicated to the pioneers and the explorers who are willing to blast into outer space, design and test their own car or even rock out with the Guardians of the Galaxy on a one-of-a-kind coaster.

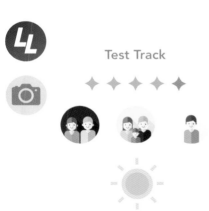

If you suffer from ANY level of motion sickness, this is not the ride for you. Despite this attraction offering a less and more intense option, neither option is particularly comfortable. If you do choose to ride, I always recommend starting on the green option.

World Showcase

Focussing on eleven cultures from around the world, Disney has done a great job of adding attractions that enlighten the experience of these cultures. Some feature characters you're familiar with and others are movies that actually show you the country from a moment in time.

Grand Fiesta Tour

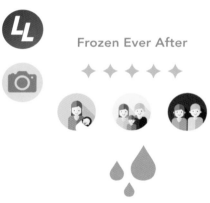

Frozen Ever After

FUN FACT

The red telephone boxes in the UK pavilion used to be functioning phone boxes with their own phone numbers. However, Disney had to disconnect them after never-ending prank calls to unsuspecting guests.

Wondrous China

American Adventure

Remy's Ratatouille Adventure

Beauty and the Beast: Sing-Along

Impressions De France

Canada Far and Wide

PRO TIP

If you arrive at Epcot for rope drop, most guests will rush to either Guardians of Galaxy: Cosmic Rewind, Test Track, Remy's Ratatouille Adventure or Frozen Ever After. My advice: head to Soarin' Around the World, Living with the Land, Journey into Imagination and The Seas. These can all get 30+ minute waits during the day, but at rope drop, you'll walk straight on each one. A great way to start your day!

Dining

If you're looking for good eats, Epcot is the place to be. With more than 10 pavilions offering food from around the world, with a variety of quick service and table service dining options, you'll never be far away from good food.

Quick Service Dining

Epcot is the best place for quick service dining that's beyond burgers and fries. At Epcot, you'll find options in each World Showcase pavilion. You could get Chinese, fish & chips, sushi and a burger, all in one park.

A great way to plan your quick service meals is to check out the menus on the MDE app ahead of your arrival.

Katsura Grill

Quite possibly my favourite quick service in all of Walt Disney World. This off-the-beaten-track location offers beautiful scenery in it's outdoor seating and air conditioning inside. I love the Chicken Cutlet Curry here, which is basically a Katsu curry.

Sunshine Seasons

Located in The Land pavilion, this extra large location offers multiple menus. If you've got a lot of people to cater for, this one-stop-shop should make everyone happy. It's also a very good place to wait out a storm if you get a table before the heavens open.

Les Halles Boulangerie-Patisserie

Nestled in the France pavilion is a wonderful bakery. Serving everything from delicate pastries, through to warm sandwiches; this is a great place for brunch. This opens before the rest of the showcase, so it's great if you're coming in through International Gateway.

Regal Eagle Smokehouse

Sometimes, you just want a cheeseburger. Regal Eagle offers ample seating and a good half-way spot along the World Showcase. This is a great spot to kick-back, enjoy some air conditioning and get a great burger. If you're looking for a meaty meal, you'll find it here.

Table Service Dining

Similar to that of quick service, the table service options at Epcot are all very different. You'll be able to find at least one table service location that's just right for you. Reservations are less often a necessity in Epcot but are always recommended.

Tepan Edo

This is the place to be if you're looking for dinner and a show. At Tepan Edo, Japanese chefs will cook your food in front of you whilst also entertaining you along the way. As groups are seated together, it's a nice place to meet other guests if you're flying solo.

Via Napoli Ristorante Pizzeria

Families, look no further than the Italy pavilion for one of the best meals of your holiday. I love my pizza and Via Napoli hasn't disappointed me yet! It offers giant pizzas fit for the whole family and a wonderful design. This is somewhere you should book ahead.

Garden Grill

Garden Grill is an all-you-care-to-enjoy family dining experience. Not only that, the restaurant is on a slow moving turn-table located in the middle of The Land. The three course Thanksgiving style meal comes to your table and you may just see some Disney friends too.

Coral Reef

If you're a big fan of fish, this is the restaurant for you. With floor to ceiling panoramic aquarium views, Coral Reef is one of a kind. This is a great place to keep the little ones quiet whilst they watch the fish. I'd recommend requesting a table close to the window if it's available.

FUN FACT

In the France Pavilion, you may notice a miniature version of the Eiffel Tower. This landmark actually doubles up as a lightning rod, protecting the guests below. It's also painted with a special coating that discourages birds from landing on it. If a bird were to sit on the tower, it would ruin the forced perspective trickery Disney uses to make it look bigger than it really is.

Quiet Spaces

There may come a time when the crowds are just a little too much at Epcot. This may especially be the case around national holidays and on weekend evenings during festivals. The following locations will allow you to gather yourself in a quiet and cool space.

⭐ **Canada Theatre** - Just before going into the Canada Far and Wide theatre, there's a large air conditioned waiting room. If a show has just started, this becomes a wonderfully quiet room to chill in.

⭐ **Japan Pavilion Gallery** - Located next to the amazing Mitsukoshi store, this gallery has benches to sit on, is air conditioned and oh so quiet.

⭐ **Morocco Pavilion Museum** - Behind an inconspicuous door at the front of the pavilion (on the left), is probably the best place to recover from a busy/hot day. Because of it's themed entrance, very few guests dare open the doors. There's a couple of benches inside where you can take a load off and cool down.

⭐ **Norwegian Church** - Similar to the museum in Morocco, few people know you can go inside the wooden church in Norway. Making it a lovely little quiet space to just calm down. This room doesn't have any seating however.

⭐ **Odyssey Pavilion** - Located between Test Track and the Mexico Pavilion, this indoor location offers ample seating, refreshments and best of all, it's nice and quiet. Now my favourite quiet space in the whole of Epcot.

⭐ **First Aid** - Worst comes to worst, head to First Aid located near Odyssey.

Entertainment

As part of Epcot's transformation, entertainment offerings are currently being reviewed and updated. With this in mind, keep an eye out for new offerings coming soon and know that some of the following entertainment is likely to change in time.

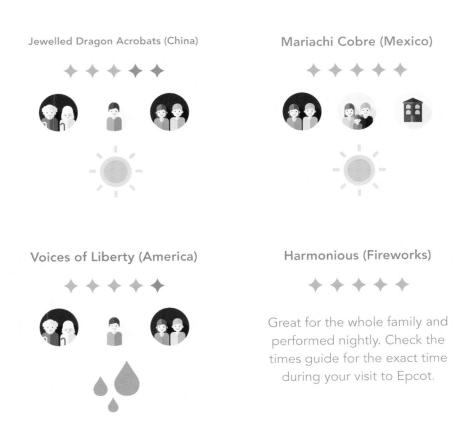

Jewelled Dragon Acrobats (China)

Mariachi Cobre (Mexico)

Voices of Liberty (America)

Harmonious (Fireworks)

Great for the whole family and performed nightly. Check the times guide for the exact time during your visit to Epcot.

Merchandise

If you're looking for shopping with a difference, you'll find a variety of international and Disney merchandise at Epcot. Below are a few recommendations if you're looking to pick-up some special souvenirs.

★ **Creations Shop** - As the main merchandise location in Epcot, Creations is pretty good at having stock when other stores on property have run out. If there's a limited edition item you're having a hard time finding, you may just find it here. The store has everything from toys to clothing and serves as one of the best one-stop-shops during your holiday. You'll find the Creations Shop in World Celebration near Spaceship Earth. You can't miss it.

★ **Mitsukoshi** - Located in the Japan pavilion, this large store celebrates the fandoms popular in Japan and culture of the country. If you like Pokémon, Hello Kitty or you'd like to try some Japanese candy, this is the store for you. There's also a fun pearl experience that allows you to pick a clam from a tank and have a small demonstration performed by the Japanese cast members.

★ **German Pavilion** - I might be cheating by saying all of the shops in the German Pavilion, but it's one of my favourite pavilions! I highly recommend checking out their cuckoo clocks, the Christmas decorations shop and I cannot recommend the Werther's confectionery enough (please try the chocolate covered strawberry).

Festivals

Throughout the year, Epcot is transformed for a variety of seasonal festivals. From mid January is the Festival of the Arts, the Flower and Garden Festival is from March until early summer, the International Food and Wine Festival kicks off in late summer, which is closely followed by Festival of the Holidays from November until the New Year.

Whilst each of these festivals are very different, there are some essential tips that apply to most, if not all of them.

* **Snack Credits** - If you've got a Disney Dining Plan as part of your trip, consider spending most of your snack credits on the festival food stalls. Whilst a snack credit typically covers something around the $5 mark, you could easily get a small dish worth $8 for one snack credit. Every credit counts when you're on a dining plan.

* **Go Early** - Locals love the festivals. They'll typically come to Epcot after 4pm. As such, World Showcase gets very busy after this time. If you're travelling with young children, I recommend completing the festival before this time. Just as some guests may become more and more inebriated.

* **Sampling Packages** - These will often allow you to try a few glasses of alcohol in different locations and save a little money compared to buying them separately. Look out for the offers posted at the registers.

Chapter 8
HOLLYWOOD STUDIOS

Disney's Hollywood Studios is the home of movie magic. Opened in 1989 as Disney MGM Studios, the park was originally designed to put you behind-the-scenes of the movies. However, the park is now designed around the idea of placing you inside the movies. With the likes of Star Wars: Galaxy's Edge, Toy Story Land and Mickey and Minnie's Runaway Railway, the park has a new lease of life which has made it one of the busiest parks day-to-day.

If you happen to have a rainy day on your holiday but still want to enjoy a day in the parks, Hollywood Studios is a great option. The park has more indoor shows than any other park and almost all attractions are either indoors or under cover. The only compromise is a limited amount of indoor dining options.

If you're travelling with teens, I would say Hollywood Studios is quite likely to be their favourite park. For little ones however, it can be limited in how much there is for them to do.

FUN FACT

The main hub of Hollywood Studios is actually one giant hidden Mickey. Take a look on Google Earth to see if you can spot him. I'll give you a hint, the lake is one of his ears.

TOP TIPS

With so many new additions to the park in recent years, you may be unfamiliar with how this park may have changed since your last visit. The following tips are designed to cover the basics of Hollywood Studios for visitors new and returning.

★ **Disney Genie+** - It's worth noting that a lot of the attractions with Genie+ Lightning Lane availability, are shows. This means rides like Slinky Dog Dash, Rock 'N' Roller Coaster and Toy Story Midway Mania, tend to have their return times depleted pretty quickly. My advice is to prioritise at Hollywood Studios, as you may only have the opportunity to Lightning Lane one or two big ticket items.

★ **Save the Shows** - If you arrive at Hollywood Studios in good time, avoid seeing any of the shows in the morning/early afternoon. The shows are a great way to cool down later in the day and rest-up. Likewise, the first few showings are normally the busiest.

★ **Fantasmic** - This is Hollywood Studios' nighttime show. Great for those that love classic Disney characters and the villains especially. The only problem with Fantasmic is that it has a limited seating capacity. This means that on busy days, you'll be pressed to get a decent view of the show if you turn up anything less than 45 minutes prior to showtime. If you can, book a Lightning Lane return time for the show.

⭐ **Dining Reservations** - Hollywood Studios is more limited in its table service dining compared to other parks. Not only are there fewer restaurants for the number of daily guests, they're a lot smaller in capacity. As such, I strongly recommend making reservations if you'd like to dine at a restaurant.

⭐ **Mornings** - With so many new attractions to enjoy, the park is incredibly popular first thing in the morning. If you're looking to line up for popular attractions like Slinky Dog Dash, Rock 'N' Roller Coaster, Millennium Falcon etc. Consider visiting after 5pm. The park gets quieter as the day goes on and lines are incredibly short just before closing (as other guests prioritise the nighttime shows).

⭐ **Fireworks -** When Hollywood Studios presents fireworks (this is not related to Fantasmic), the main firing pad is off to the right of the Chinese Theatre facade. This means, if you're standing too far back on Hollywood Boulevard, you'll miss a large portion of the fireworks. For the best view, stand in the main plaza ahead of the Keystone Clothiers store.

Attractions

From state-of-the-art immersion to fun for the whole family, Hollywood Studios has some of the best and newest rides in Walt Disney World. Whilst attractions for toddlers may be limited, most attractions accommodate children over 1.22m in height. Wait times can get long in Hollywood Studios, so this may be a good time to consider some investments in Lightning Lane options.

Mickey & Minnie's Runaway Railway

Located in the chinese theatre as you come in, this state-of-the-art attraction places the whole family right into a Mickey Mouse cartoon. It's a whole lot of fun and a must do for any Disney fan.

FUN FACT

Runaway Railway is housed in the building that formerly held The Great Movie Ride. This attraction would show guests some of the biggest scenes in Cinema history. In Runaway Railway, you can find Easter Eggs that pay tribute to this classic attraction. Look out for The Great Movie Ride poster in the carnival scene. Hint: it's near the popcorn stand.

Star Wars: Galaxy's Edge

Set in the timeline of Kylo Ren, Rey and the First Order, Galaxy's Edge is by far the most immersive land Disney has ever created. Here you can enjoy some of the food, drinks, sounds and thrills of what it's like to be in a Star Wars movie. One may argue the land itself is an attraction.

Millennium Falcon: Smugglers Run

Star Wars: Rise of Resistance

One of the best rides in history, Rise of the Resistance throws you into the action and makes you feel like you're really fighting to escape the First Order. This is pretty much three attractions in one. My advice for a shorter wait: go right at the end of the day, just before closing.

Toy Story Land

Shrink down to the size of a toy and hang out with Woody, Jessie, Buzz and the gang in Andy's backyard. This land is so brilliantly themed and colourful, it's a great place for the kids and big kids to play. You can even spot Andy's massive foot prints on the ground.

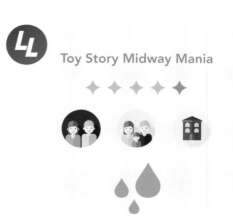

Toy Story Midway Mania

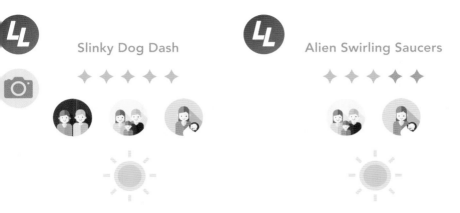

Slinky Dog Dash

Alien Swirling Saucers

FUN FACT

Cast Members in Star Wars: Galaxy's Edge are actually residents of the planet Batuu. Chat to them and see if you can learn some helpful Batuu greetings and phrases.

Sunset Boulevard

Dance back in time to the glitz and glamour of vintage Hollywood. The Hollywood Tower Hotel lingers over the street as you make your way down to two classic Hollywood Studios attractions. Look out for the citizens of Hollywood as you explore Sunset.

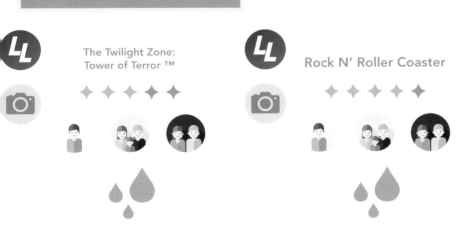

The Twilight Zone:
Tower of Terror ™

Rock N' Roller Coaster

Echo Lake, Grand Avenue & Animation Courtyard

Throughout Hollywood Studios you'll find lands that are dedicated to the magic of movies. From learning how stunt movies are made, to going behind the scenes. These three lands have a lot to discover.

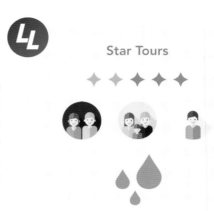

Star Tours

Muppet Vision 3D

Star Wars Launch Bay

Walt Disney Presents

If you're a Disney fan that loves learning about the history of Disney, this is a must-do; especially if you're interested in how Disney creates their world-class attractions. This is also a great place to wait out a storm or catch a sneak-peak of a new movie.

Dining

Out of all the parks, Hollywood Studios is probably the most 'American' when it comes to food. Just like the other parks, the food is part of the theming. If you love a good burger or even American home cooking, this is where to be. Dining options are somewhat limited for the size of the park, so plan ahead with your Mobile Orders and dining reservations.

Quick Service Dining

As there's a limited number of table service locations and they're each pretty small, the quick service locations tend to be the best bet for most families at Hollywood Studios.

With that in mind, if there's a day you can dine outside of the busy meal periods, this is the day to do it. Lunch is especially busy at quick service restaurants.

Backlot Express

If, like me, you enjoy Disney french fries and chicken nuggets, this is a great option. With a refillable drinks machine and large selection of indoor seating, it's a great place to take a load off. Indoor seating is limited however, so avoid busy times if you need some air-con.

ABC Commissary

If you're a fan of ABC shows, pop into this quick service for at least a look around. Every so often you'll find props and costumes from some of your favourite ABC TV shows. Seating here can get a little limited when it's lunchtime. Outside of then, it's a great place to cool down.

Sunset Ranch Market

If you're looking for a pick-me-up or you've got a lot of people to feed that all want something different, make your way to Sunset Ranch Market. With multiple snack and lunch options, it's a great place to please everyone. Just know all the seating is outdoors.

Table Service Dining

The great thing about the table service options here, is that they're all a little different. As I mentioned earlier, due to the size of the restaurants and how few there are, it's not always easy to get in for lunch or dinner without a reservation. For that reason, be sure to book ahead.

Mama Melrose's

Now one of my favourite theme park restaurants, Mama Melrose's has a very nice family feel about it. Fantastic American-Italian food served in a warm environment that I'd definitely recommend for large families. Additionally, the restaurant is a nice break from the busy park.

Hollywood Brown Derby

Honestly one my favourite dining experiences in Disney and a really great choice for a date-night. Exceptional service standards, great food and a replica of the Brown Derby in Hollywood, featuring celebrity caricatures all over the walls. I recommend the steak.

Sci-Fi Dine-In

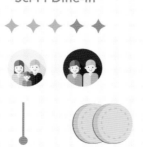

This restaurant is something right out of a 50's movie! Designed like a drive-in movie theatre, you'll dine in cars. I wouldn't recommend this restaurant if you have an odd number of guests (someone may be sat by themselves) or a large party (as there's limited large tables).

Entertainment

If you like a show, you're going to love Hollywood Studios! Boasting more than eight entertainment experiences, you'll have plenty of choice when it comes to a little bit of show-time. I'd recommend getting to shows approximately 20-30 minutes prior to the scheduled start time. Theatres can fill up quickly on hot days with guests trying to get some invaluable air-conditioning time.

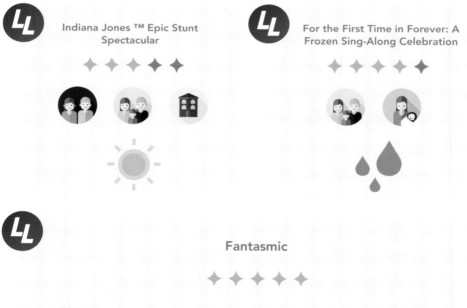

Indiana Jones ™ Epic Stunt Spectacular

For the First Time in Forever: A Frozen Sing-Along Celebration

Fantasmic

This show reaches capacity pretty much every evening. As such, I recommend arriving 45-60 minutes prior to showtime. Even with a Lighting Lane return time, a great view isn't guaranteed. For a guaranteed great view, consider a Fantasmic dining package.

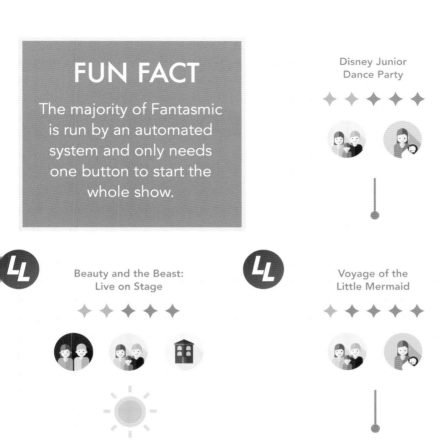

FUN FACT

The majority of Fantasmic is run by an automated system and only needs one button to start the whole show.

Disney Junior Dance Party

Beauty and the Beast: Live on Stage

Voyage of the Little Mermaid

Star Wars Building/Entertainment Experiences

If you've got a big Star Wars fan in your travel party, they may be interested in building their own Lightsaber at Savi's Workshop, or their own droid at the Droid Depot. The Lightsaber experience is great, but expensive. It currently costs $220 +tax, and the droid experience is $99.99 +tax. Each experience is the cost of one builder and one companion (who can watch).

Whilst there's occasionally walk-up availability, these experiences are normally always fully booked. You can book your reservation online, or by calling:

+1 407-WDW-PLAY

Merchandise

From Star Wars souvenirs to homeware, Hollywood Studios has got some great options for treating yourself. Merchandise stores are considerably smaller than compared to the other parks, so I recommend trying to do your shopping mid-afternoon when most guests are busy with the rides.

★ **Celebrity 5 & 10** - Located on the right hand side of Hollywood Boulevard as you come in, this is one of the best stores for finding real treasures. I can't tell you how many times I've been in this store and found something I haven't seen anywhere else.

★ **Legends of Hollywood** - Located on the corner of Sunset Boulevard and Hollywood Boulevard, this jewellery shop has some great one-of-a-kind pieces, as well as items from Pandora.

★ **Dok-Ondar's Den of Antiquities** - Selling legacy Lightsabers, Kyber Crystals for Lightsabers and unique Star Wars artefacts, this store is a must for any Star Wars fan. Even just looking around this store is something really cool! Look out for Dok-Ondar himself as he works in the shop tinkering at his work station.

Quiet Spaces

Quiet spaces are a little harder to come-by in Hollywood Studios, especially if you're looking for a sit-down out of the heat. However, here are a few little sweet spots that can get you out of the hustle and bustle and into some air conditioning.

⭐ **Walt Disney Presents** - Possibly the best place in the park to take a quiet 15, with gentle Disney music playing in the background, it's a lovely place to have a little browse. There's also a screening you can enjoy before re-entering into the park.

⭐ **Stage 1 Company Store** - Located in the Grand Avenue area, providing there's not a Muppets Vision 3D show letting out, it's a good spot to stop.

⭐ **ABC Commissary** - Outside of main dining times, this quick service restaurant is both air-conditioned, spacious and quiet.

⭐ **First Aid** - Located at the front of the park, the first aid center will be able to assist if everything gets a bit 'much' for anyone.

⭐ **Star Wars Launch Bay** - Located on the opposite side of the park from Galaxy's Edge, this is the meet & greet location for popular Star Wars characters like Darth Vader and BB-8. However, the venue offers lots of space to chill out. There's also plenty of Star Wars memorabilia/props if you're looking to geek-out whilst you take some time out.

⭐ **Pizza Rizzo** - Whilst only open during peak seasons, this quick service restaurant offers a spacious upstairs dining room that's far quieter than other dining locations in the park.

Chapter 9
ANIMAL KINGDOM

If you're looking for a real-life escape from reality, look no further than Animal Kingdom. There are few places where I genuinely forget where I am; this however is one of them.

At Animal Kingdom, theming, dining, music and animals allow you to disappear into different continents and other worlds entirely.

Whilst Animal Kingdom never fails to feel like the hottest place on the planet, it's also the park I'm often most excited to get back to. The amount of detail Imagineers put into this park is visible at every turn.

It isn't simply a zoo... It's a place where creative storytelling explores the beauty of animals alongside world-class attractions and shows. Whether it's a show celebrating the animals featured in the Lion King or a trail that leads you into the habitat of gorillas, Animal Kingdom has adventures for everyone. Not to mention, the incredibly popular Pandora: The World of Avatar.

FUN FACT

The Tree of Life is Animal Kingdom's icon. It's made up of over 300 beautiful animal carvings that all intertwine with one another. You can get a better look on the walking trail.

TOP TIPS

The park's unique design is all meant to evoke exploration and adventure. Whilst it may be a little puzzling to navigate on your first visit, you'll find some tips below that will help any visitor prepare for their day at Animal Kingdom.

* **Heat & Humidity** - Because of where the park is built, when it's hot, it feels even hotter here. Not only that, the park is packed with trees and foliage. Whilst beautiful, they have a nasty habit of trapping the heat and humidity. With this, be sure to wear light and breathable clothing and make time for regular rest within air conditioned locations. A handheld fan may also be a worthy investment.

* **Pandora: The World of Avatar** - Opened in 2017, this land remains one of the biggest draws across the whole of Walt Disney World. It's a good idea to know ahead of time that this area of the park is extremely busy from opening until close. If you're without Lightning Lane return times for either attraction, I recommend getting in line as soon as the park opens or when the park is about to close.

* **Disney Genie+** - If you're purchasing Genie+ day-by-day, Animal Kingdom is where I'd advise against purchasing it. With less than six Lightning Lane attractions in the whole park, it's very difficult to get good use out of the $15 per person. An Individual Attraction Selection for Flight of Passage however, may be worth the money for you.

★ **Animal Activity** - If you're planning to see some animals whilst at Animal Kingdom (which I hope you are), then get to the park as early as possible. If you choose to take a walk along the trails or ride Kilimanjaro Safaris in the morning, you're much more likely to see the animals up and about. Two factors add into this, it's cooler and they've only recently been fed.

★ **Flash Pictures** - When visiting Animal Kingdom, take the courtesy of switching off your flash for the day. Without thinking, you'll be snapping away and may forget the discomfort your camera's flash may have on the animals. This also applies to other guests on Na'vi River Journey.

★ **Nighttime** - Since Disney introduced nighttime entertainment at the park, evenings have gone from quiet to quieter in regard to attractions. After the sun's gone down, head for attractions like Dinosaur, Expedition Everest and Flight of Passage. I warn you now however, Expedition Everest at night is not for the faint hearted. I'm not sure how, but the dark makes it so much more thrilling!

★ **Tree Awakening** - At the end of your evening at Animal Kingdom, stop-by the Tree of Life and just wait. Every 15 minutes or so, the tree magically awakens with beautiful lighting and projections. There are multiple stories to the awakenings too, so you can easily enjoy a few shows before heading out.

★ **Strollers & ECVs** - If there's a park you'd like to try not using a stroller or ECV, I strongly recommend Animal Kingdom for this. With uneven paths and thin promenades, even quiet days can seem a little congested. At busy times, navigating the park without either is still difficult.

Attractions

Whilst you won't be spoilt for choice, almost every attraction has something unique over others you may have been on. Where else in the world can you fly on the back of a fictional alien beast?

The great thing about Animal Kingdom, is that in the absence of attractions, there are animals. I highly recommend taking the time to enjoy some of the beautiful walking trails and animal exhibits.

PRO TIP

Pack your rain gear for Animal Kingdom. There are few attractions that offer an escape from the rain if the heavens open. If you come prepared, you'll be able to continue enjoying your day.

Discovery Island

Home of the world famous Tree of Life that towers over the park, Discovery Island is just beyond your welcome to the park.

From Discovery Island you'll be able to venture into the various lands that make up Disney's Animal Kingdom.

It's Tough to be a Bug!

Discovery Island Trails

Pandora: The World of Avatar

By far the most popular land of Animal Kingdom, it's a sight to be seen. With two of the best rides across all of Walt Disney World and some of the best theming seen in the theme park industry, even just walking through this land is an attraction in itself.

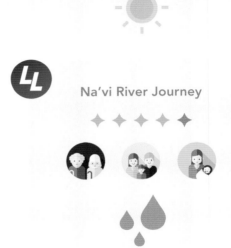

Na'vi River Journey

Avatar: Flight of Passage

Africa

Inspired by the architecture, music and nature of Africa, this is my favourite area of the park for themeing. Especially at night, Africa has a certain air about it with the unique lighting and subtle music. Look out for the live musicians during the day, they add a whole lot of energy to the area!

Gorilla Falls Exploration Trail

Kilimanjaro Safaris

Asia

Asian food, attractions and animals await in this detailed area of the park. From the jungle through to the Himalayan mountains, this land is incredibly detailed and offers you plenty of exploration opportunities.

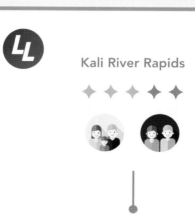

Kali River Rapids

Expedition Everest

Maharajah Jungle Trek

Dinoland U.S.A

Certainly the more kid-friendly area of the park, this land features fantastic character meet and greets, play grounds and a fun fair style theme if you're looking to try your luck on some carnival games. The main attraction DINOSAUR however, may be scary for little ones.

DINOSAUR

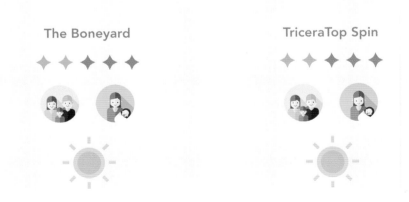

The Boneyard

TriceraTop Spin

Dining

Whilst Animal Kingdom is the largest park, a lot of that space is occupied by animals and attractions. Whilst big, it doesn't have as much choice as Magic Kingdom and Epcot when it comes to food.

Quick Service Dining

As I mentioned earlier, Animal Kingdom tends to feel the hottest. Part of that is due to the few locations that actually offer indoor seating and air-conditioning.

That being said, Animal Kingdom has a couple of quick service locations that, whilst outdoors, offer some of the best affordable in-park food. These locations are popular so Mobile Order ahead.

Restaurantosaurus

If you're in a pinch and just in need of burgers and fries, you're in luck with this quick-service. Offering plenty of indoor seating, this is a great location for taking a break outside of busy dining periods. This should also be a good place for any picky eaters in the family.

Satu'li Canteen

Offering a selection of bowl dishes in which you can choose your base, meat and topping, this is a quick-service restaurant with a difference. Not only is the food pretty good, the ceiling boasts beautiful hand woven Na'vi artwork which adds a unique beauty to the location.

Harambe Market

If you're looking for choice and food with a bit of culture mixed in, look no further than Harambe Market. With multiple choices and plenty of seating, it's a popular spot to grab lunch. However, shade can be hard to come-by, so I wouldn't go here if it's hot.

Yak & Yeti

If you're a fan of Chinese food, make your way to the Yak & Yeti quick service location. My personal favourite here is the honey chicken dish. If you've got a gap to fill but don't want a full meal, the chicken fried rice does a good job of filling that void.

Table Service Dining

There are far fewer table service dining options in Animal Kingdom. They're also a bit hit or miss. I've had great and also not so great. For more certainty in your table service dining, I would recommend planning to eat at a resort hotel restaurant or Disney Springs after your day.

Tiffins

Some of the best food I've had in Disney and truly outstanding service. The interior design of this restaurant encompasses hundreds of pieces of art collected by Imagineers whilst they conducted research for the development of Animal Kingdom.

Tusker House

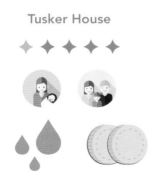

Whilst I didn't like my dining experience at Tusker House, it's a favourite of many. This is a character dining buffet and whilst I found it a little too loud and close for my liking, I'm aware families love it. I'd recommend going for breakfast based on the feedback I've heard.

Entertainment

As well as the following sit-down shows, you'll be able to find a variety of small pop-up performances around the park. These may range from live bands to dance acts. These pop-ups really add to the atmosphere of Animal Kingdom. Whilst it may be tempting to just keep heading to the next ride, I really recommend stopping to enjoy these shows and soaking up the fun.

Kite Tails

UP! A Great Bird Adventure

Finding Nemo - The Musical

Festival of the Lion King

Merchandise

Shopping at Animal Kingdom is a little different from the other parks. Whilst you'll find the main souvenir stores at the front of the park on Discovery Island, a lot of the shopping opportunities are spaced out in small locations. You're more likely to find something special in the smaller locations. For example, Serka Zong Bazaar at the exit of Expedition Everest has some great finds.

Animals

Throughout the park, you'll find a variety of Animal enclosures. Disney has done a great job of weaving the animals in and around the park to really bring the park to life. However, there's been a careful consideration as to where the animals are placed within the park to ensure they're not disrupted by a roller coaster whizzing by every 60 seconds.

Quiet Spaces

With the heat at Animal Kingdom and thinner than normal paths, it's a good idea to take a little break when you can.

⭐ **Tamu Tamu** - This small quick service location in Africa has some lovely shaded seating which is quiet outside of meal times.

⭐ **Nomad Lounge** - Next door to Tiffins, this is your go-to relaxing space. Whilst you may have to get a drink, it's a comfortable lounge to chill in.

⭐ **Rafiki's Planet Watch** - If you want to really feel like you've got out of the park, head to Rafiki's Planet Watch by the train located in Africa. This secluded area features benches, shade and even goats.

Chapter 10
DISNEY SPRINGS

Welcome to one of my favourite places in Walt Disney World. Whilst living in Florida, Disney Springs was my happy place. Whenever I had an afternoon or evening free, I'd be here soaking up the atmosphere.

Disney Springs is a shopping, dining and entertainment village located outside of the parks. It's free to enter and buses take you to and from your resort hotel.

Formally known as Downtown Disney, Disney Springs features; high street, high-end and exclusive shopping. It has plenty of snack, quick service and table service dining locations, as well as a multiplex cinema, bowling alley, Cirque Du Soleil show and live entertainment nightly.

No matter where you're staying, Disney Springs is worth one or two visits during your holiday. With some of the best eats in the Orlando area, it's well worth your time popping over for an evening.

TOP TIPS

There's so much to see and do at Disney Springs, I could write an entire book on all the places you could enjoy. Even if you spent two weeks just at Disney Springs, you still couldn't try it all! Here's some top tips for a visit.

* **Parking** - First of all, it's FREE! So even if you're staying off-property, there's no reason to hesitate visiting even for an hour or two. Secondly, Disney has employed a digital parking system that will show you how many spaces are free on each level. Not only that, a green beacon will appear over any empty spaces. With an updated road system, it's easy to get in and out of Disney Springs quickly.

* **Boat Service** - To help you get around, boats service the three main areas of the property. Whilst these services may typically take longer than walking, if you're going from Marketplace to West Side, it'll save you one heck of a walk.

* **What Can You Get Elsewhere?** - One of the biggest mistakes guests make at Disney Springs, is dining at places they've heard of before. Rainforest Cafe, for example, is one of the busiest locations, but really, you can find one in every major city. As such, I recommend trying some Disney Springs exclusives.

* **Shopping Mornings** - If it's stores like Sephora, Kate Spade and Zara exciting you to take a trip to Disney Springs, choose to visit in the morning when the stores open at 9am. It's considerably quieter before lunchtime.

Dining

If it's food you're after, you'll be spoilt for choice at Disney Springs. With a large variety of quick service and table service options, there's something for every budget and preference. If you're struggling for what to do and know you need to get lunch/dinner, there's a good chance you'll find what you're craving here.

Quick Service Dining

These options are incredibly popular at Disney Springs. Whilst they're called 'quick' service, due to the lines at most of these locations, don't expect to be in and out in a flash. Similar to the parks, if you can avoid those peak dining hours, it'll save you a lot of time when you're enjoying your time here. If there's a long line, chances are it's somewhere worth waiting for. Here are my top eats:

Chicken Guy

By far one of the most popular and affordable options at Disney Springs. Serving up the best chicken tenders you'll ever eat and more sauces than you can shake a stick at, this is one of my favourites. Evening's can be pretty busy here, so I'd recommend visiting for lunch.

Blaze Pizza

Think Subway, but with Pizza. Here you can choose every element of your own pizza. Not only is it incredibly flexible to what each person in your party wants, it's super cheap! You're looking at less than $15 a person here, making it the best for value in my opinion.

D-Luxe Burger

I hope you're ready to have the best burger of your life! It's pricier than other quick service restaurants but it's 100% worth it. Whilst often busy, there's a reason. The line to order often moves pretty slowly. As such, this is a great time to utilise Mobile Order (page 79).

Earl of Sandwich

The home of amazing hot sandwiches. If you're looking for a place to please the whole family, visit Earl of Sandwich. With an extensive menu of hot sandwiches, wraps and salads, this is a great affordable lunch. The Holiday Turkey sandwich is my favourite.

Table Service Dining

We've got table service options coming out of our ears at Disney Springs. Having tried a lot of them (not all of them) I've picked out some of my favourites. If you're trying to dine at places you can't find elsewhere, these should be some great one-of-a-kind options.

Jaleo

Possibly the freshest tapas I've ever had, if you don't mind trying new foods, Jaleo is a must! The culinary team here starts as early as 4:30am to start prepping the freshest organic food. The exceptional attention to detail is even in the bread that's flown in from Spain!

Frontera Cocina

I LOVE Mexican food. It's also one of the only things I can cook consistently well. However, not as well as the chefs at Frontera Cocina! If you're looking to try some of the menu before investing in a full meal, consider getting a snack from the quick service window on the side.

Chef Art Smith's Homecomin'

If you like fried chicken and southern style hospitality, look no further than Homecomin'. I had to go back here a couple of times the food and atmosphere were so good. I'd recommend this location if you're partial to an alcoholic beverage or two.

The Boathouse

Great food and great service. Every single cast member at this location was on it. Everyone greeted us, our server was possibly the best I'd ever had and everyone wished us well when we left. The only downside was waiting for our table and the proximity to other guests.

Snacks & Speciality

Whilst it's great to grab a meal in Disney Springs, there's a couple of fly-by places you simply have to try! There's a lot of small kiosk style eats around the property, so you'll never be far away from a quick snack or drink. However, the two below are places I have down as must-dos.

Sprinkles

Sweet tooth? Well, get ready to try the best cupcake ever! Everyone I've taken here for the first time has had the same look of pure euphoria as they bite into their first frosted Sprinkles cupcake. They even have a cupcake vending machine outside. Salted Caramel's my fave.

Coca-Cola Store

All that eating and shopping might have taken it out of you. Well, there's no better place to chill out than the roof-top bar at the *Coca-cola* store. This is where you can sample various *Coca-Cola* products from around the world and just enjoy a sunny day.

Shopping

Welcome to shopaholic heaven. If like me, it doesn't take a lot to enable you into a purchase, only take a certain amount of money with you to Disney Springs. Below, you'll find some of my favourites shops:

⭐ **Sephora** - If you're from the UK and love make-up, I know you're already cracking your knuckles ready for this store. With a great selection of make-up and skin-care products you can't find everywhere, it's a great place for international visitors. Here, you can pick up products that are just too expensive to ship home. The staff are always super friendly, they know their stuff and they're more than happy to recommend products for you.

⭐ **365 Days of Christmas** - If you're up for a bit of festive cheer (no matter the time of year) pop by the Days of Christmas store at the far end of Disney Springs Marketplace. Not only does it smell of festive goodness, but you can also find some special ornaments to prep yourself for the Christmas season or even get a personalised bauble.

⭐ **Art of Disney** - Just across the way from the Days of Christmas store is the best place for Disney art and graphic pieces. It's also where you can find the original paintings that are replicated across property. If there's a particular character you or a friend likes, you can get a custom drawing done of the character of your choosing. Maybe something special for an upcoming birthday?

⭐ **UNIQLO** - If you're missing some essentials (e.g. vests, t-shirts etc.) this is the place to pick them up at an affordable price. Not only that, they have a great Disney selection. The selection tends to change pretty regularly so if you see something you like, I suggest getting it then and there. As this store has so much footfall, it can sometimes be difficult to find items in your size.

Chapter 11
DREAM GUIDE TO MORE

By now, you should already know Walt Disney World is big! There's so much fun to be had in your resort hotel and in the parks. However, when you're spending a week or two in the Orlando area, there's also so much beyond the Disney parks.

In this chapter, I'm going to take you through some of my favourite things to do beyond the parks. A lot of families get into the habit of sticking to what they know. This should helpfully show you what you may be missing out on.

Disney Resorts

Fort Wilderness Campfire - Roast smores by a campfire whilst Chip and Dale host a special sing-along. Then, enjoy a Disney movie on the big open-air screen. As long as it's not due to rain, head to the Meadow Depot area for this FREE experience (smores kits cost about $10). To get to the venue when you arrive at Fort Wilderness, take an internal bus on either the yellow or orange route.

Circle D Ranch - If anyone in your party likes horses, make time to visit the stables at The Settlement at Fort Wilderness. I recommend going in the afternoon for the chance to speak to the cast members and maybe even get a tour of the stables. There are even ponny rides for little ones. Prices start at $8 for one lap.

Hoop-Dee-Doo Musical Revue - The dinner show of all dinner shows! Having been a number of times, this dinner show at Fort Wilderness is well worth your time. Whilst not cheap, it's worth the money! Pro-tip: if you go to the later show and book a cheaper seat, if the show isn't full, you may just get a free upgrade (not guaranteed).

Fireworks from the Polynesian Village Resort - Just across the Seven Seas Lagoon from Magic Kingdom is the Polynesian Village. If you fancy seeing some fireworks but don't want the hustle and bustle of the parks, stop-by the Polynesian beach at showtime. You get a great view of the fireworks from across the lagoon, and there's some great places to get drinks and snacks. I personally recommend the Spikey Pineapple from the terrace bar if you like Dole Whip.

Grand Floridian Music - Visit Disney's Grand Floridian resort after 4pm for your chance to enjoy the live pianist. If you'd like a date night, the Grand is the place to be. Adorn some of your fancy attire for fine-dining at the newly refurbished Citricos, enjoy casual dining at the Grand Floridan Cafe or unwind with cocktails at the Enchanted Rose bar as you let the night slip away.

River Roost - Located at Port Orleans Riverside, on select nights through the week, you can enjoy a piano show unlike any other. Most popular with regulars of the resort, you'll want to get there ahead of the show starting to even be in the chance of scoring a table. Even if you're not staying at the resort, it's something fun for the whole family and the quick service there is amazing.

Water Parks

In Orlando, you've got four main water parks to choose from. At Disney, you'll find Typhoon Lagoon and Blizzard Beach. Sea World runs Aquatica and at Universal, you've got Volcano Bay. If you had to choose from one and you're going to be paying for your entry, I'd recommend Volcano Bay as it's by far my favourite.

However, if you're visiting Disney and have their water parks included in your ticket, I don't think it's worth paying extra to go to other water parks. Here are some tips to help you get the most out of whichever water park you go to.

★ **Towels** - It costs to rent towels at the water parks. With that in mind, if you're staying at a Disney resort hotel, stop-by your pool to pick-up some complimentary towels and take them with you.

★ **Go Early** - Especially if visiting Volcano Bay at Universal, go for opening. Not only do they sometimes reach capacity, but the heat will be much kinder to your feet as you walk around the park.

★ **Slides** - If you're visiting Blizzard Beach in particular, know some of the slides aren't the most comfortable. The grooves in the slide tend to hurt after a while and so I mostly stick to the rubber ring or mat slides.

★ **Hydrate** - It's so important to drink water at the water parks. As you're in and out of water, you can sometimes forget how hot it really is. Especially when you're climbing stairs and swimming all day.

★ **MagicBands** - If you haven't linked a credit card to your MagicBand, a water park day is a good day to do so. You can then buy food and drinks without having to go back to your locker.

Orlando Dining

With Orlando attracting millions of visitors annually, there are plenty of places to eat outside of Disney.

If you want to go off property one night, maybe to save a dining credit for a signature location or you're renting a villa, these are some of my favourite off property restaurants.

* **Cheesecake Factory** - Not far from Universal is Mall at Millennia. There you'll find the Cheesecake Factory. It's probably the biggest menu you'll ever find and the portions are crazy! Just note, the wait is normally pretty long.

* **BJ's Brewhouse** - If you want a lot of choice but don't want to stray too far from Disney, BJ's is the place for you. This was a typical haunt for my colleagues and I after a long day at work. Lots of choice and not too pricey.

* **Saffron Indian Cuisine** - For us Brits, a curry is as British as fish & chips. I made it one of my missions to find a decent curry house in Orlando and I believe I found it! The papadams miss the mark but everything else is ace.

* **Olive Garden** - Whilst American's won't consider Olive Garden anything special, to us Brits, it's heaven! The bread sticks, the portion sizes, the Italian theme and the value for money, all make it a British holiday favourite.

* **Panera Bread** - My personal favourite destination for breakfast or lunch off property. With soups in bread bowls, hot sandwiches and a great bakery selection, it's affordable and different from locations in Disney.

Universal Studios

Whilst beyond the gates of Disney, Universal Orlando Resort is worth at least one of your days if you've never been to Florida before or if you've been to Disney a couple of times. My advice for a visit to Universal, is to not compare it to Disney like-for-like. If you like thrills and 3D, you're bound to have a great day at their two theme parks.

Getting There - If you're staying at Disney, it can often be a tricky business knowing exactly how to get to Universal. In my experience, I've found ride share services like *Lyft* and *Uber* are the most convenient and the most affordable.

PRO TIP

Order your ride share to and from one of Universal's hotels (especially during busy times). You'll have a much more pleasant experience entering/ leaving the resort this way.

Dining - Whilst I struggle to find decent quick service meals at Universal, there are some great table service options on City Walk and at the resort hotels. In City Walk, Hard Rock Cafe is one of my favourites, as is Bubba Gump's and Panda Express. At Portofino Bay there's the incredible Mama Della's, and The Kitchen at the Hard Rock Hotel.

Express Pass - For approximately $110 per person, Universal offers unlimited access to their express lines for a whole day. If you're staying at one of the luxury Universal hotels, this is included as part of your stay. Whilst pricey, Express Passes can be worth it for a single day visit to make sure you get on everything.

Lockers - It's important to know ahead of time, you can't take bags on most Universal attractions. Some attractions will even require you to empty your pockets and pass through metal detection before riding. Small lockers are provided for free at each of these attractions and can just about fit a standard back-pack in them. There are larger lockers available, but these come with a fee.

Motion Sickness - If like me, you find motion simulators a little 'much,' really consider whether a ride is suitable for you. With so many rides featuring motion simulators and 3D, one ride could ruin your day if it makes you feel unwell. The worst offenders for me are The Simpsons Ride, Transformers: The Ride, Race Through New York and Spider-man: The Ride.

2 Park Pass - Can you do two parks in one day? Yes. Should you? Yes. You can spend a number of days in Universal but if you just want to 'do it,' you'll easily be able to catch the highlights in both parks with a one day, 2 park ticket.

Hagrid's Motorbike Adventure - Still unbeaten as my favourite ride/roller coaster in the whole world, this is the world's first story-coaster. Using state-of-the-art technology, seven launches and multiple ride systems, this is one attraction you will not want to miss (no matter how long the wait is).

Water Rides - The water rides at Universal will get you wet. VERY wet. With that in mind, dress accordingly or bring a change of clothes to avoid squelching for the rest of your day.

PRO TIP

Buy your tickets online and collect from a will-call kiosk to save time. If needing to purchase at the gate, do so at Islands of Adventure.

Tours

I love learning about how the Disney parks operate. I find it so interesting to see how Walt's ideas materialised into what we get to enjoy today.

Across property are a variety of tours that will allow you to see everything from how the Christmas decorations come to life, to how Disney look after the animals at Animal Kingdom.

Whilst the tours can be pricey, I'd say they're worth every penny for the service and experience. You can book a tour via the main booking line which is currently

+1 407-WDW-PLAY (+1 407-939-8687)

My favourite tours include:

Keys to the Kingdom - An all day tour that allows you to see how Magic Kingdom operates behind the scenes.

Be warned, this is a long walking tour. On the tour you'll get to see inside the utilidoor (the tunnels underneath Magic Kingdom that cast members use to get around), enjoy a couple of rides with your tour guide and it includes a quick service lunch.

Marceline to Magic - Probably the best value tour, this Magic Kingdom walking tour shows you how Walt went from Marceline Missouri, to creating the world of Disney we enjoy today.

This lasts approximately three hours and will allow you to see how the ghosts in Haunted Mansion work, as well as a guided tour of Main Street U.S.A. and a ride on Carousel of Progress.

Wilk Africa Trek - One of the best things I've ever done in my life! Not only are the cast that conduct this tour beyond amazing, the tour itself offers you the chance to rope bridge (weather permitting) over Nile Crocodile, learn about the animals and dine in the middle of the savannah.

If you choose to do this tour and, like me, there's a few things you don't like to eat (e.g. shellfish), mention this when checking in for your tour. Your meal out on the Savannah has to be prepared in advance.

Boating - Not exactly a tour, but from select hotels you can take a small speedboat or even a pontoon out on the lakes around Walt Disney World.

I'd recommend packing a picnic and taking a pontoon out from the Grand Floridian. It's a nice way to explore both Bay Lake and Seven Seas Lagoon. You don't need any qualifications or boating experience, you'll be given a demonstration before setting off and lifeguards are on-hand around the lakes.

Wanyama Safari - Run at Animal Kingdom Lodge, this is a tour for those of you looking to enjoy some fine dining as well as a guided safari.

I'd say this tour is on the more luxurious side and is a lot more sociable than the other tours I've experienced. Your group is made to feel like one big family, as you enjoy a 45-60 minute tour of the savannahs at the lodge, followed by a family-style tasting meal at Jiko.

Dessert Parties

To enhance your trip, you may want to consider a dessert party. Normally attached to a fireworks show, these ticketed experiences allow you to indulge in an all-you-care-to-enjoy buffet (mainly consisting of desserts) and unlimited beer, wine, cocktails, mocktails and soft drinks. Prices for dessert parties vary but $60-100 per person is a good guide.

Are they worth the money? Well, it depends on what you're hoping to get out of them. If you're looking for a guaranteed good view of a show you haven't seen before, then yes, they're worth their weight in gold. However, if you're looking for a buffet that'll replace your evening meal, it may be worth considering an alternative.

In my experience, dessert parties are something special. If you're celebrating someone's birthday, an anniversary, engagement etc. Then a dessert party is a great way to mark the occasion. To book a dessert party, call:

+1 407 WDW-PLAY (+1 407 939 7529)

FUN FACT

Disney fires off their fireworks with compressed air cannons. These reduce the amount of smoke their spectaculars produce.

Outlets & Malls

If you're looking for retail therapy, Orlando's got you covered. From malls showcasing only the finest of designer labels, to outlets that'll help you find a mega deal, you can shop until you drop.

In fact, on every trip I take to Disney, I'll put aside at least one day for going shopping. Mainly as I can save a pretty penny buying my clothes state-side.

⭐ **Mall at Millennia** - Located near Universal Studios, this mall is best for designer stores (full price).

⭐ **Florida Mall** - Ideal for a more varied shopping experience, you'll find more choice here if you're looking to kill some time.

⭐ **Premium Outlets: Vineland Avenue** - Not too far from Disney, this outlet mall is where I'd recommend going at least once on your trip. Mainly for Character Warehouse (a discounted Disney Parks merchandise store) but also for Pop-Bar, an amazing frozen yogurt lolly stand that is just everything!

Index

Acknowledgements

By holding this book in your hand, you have played a role in allowing me to do what I love. For that, I am forever grateful. Whether you've watched my vlogs on YouTube or just ordered this book on a whim, thank you so so much. I truly hope you have the most wonderful time in Walt Disney World and that some of my tips can help make your trip even more magical.

It's only with the help of my friend Gary C, did I have such wonderful pictures to include in this Dream Guide. Without Gary, I honestly wouldn't be where I am today. Being his friend has allowed me to grow personally and professionally with a guardian angel by my side. So thank you Gary; I couldn't have done this book without you. Your friendship, kindness and support, is all I need to get through the bad days and thrive on the good days.

To my Mum, thank you for giving me a home and environment that allowed my creativity to run wild as a kid. To grow up thinking only the sky was the limit, allowed me to think 'maybe I can,' even on days when I thought I couldn't. And to my Stepdad, your opinion means so much to me and I appreciate your advice no end. I'm so lucky to have parents as amazing as you both and I thank you for giving me the gumption to reach for the stars.

Finally, to Walt. You created worlds that allowed people to escape their reality, immerse themselves in your story-telling and just enjoy being happy for a moment. Whether for the length of a movie or a two week holiday, the building blocks you put in place bring untold joy to myself and millions of guests every year. Without you, I wouldn't have met my best friends, I wouldn't have my career and I wouldn't have had the pleasure of connecting with thousands of people around the world, all through our common love of the stories you told. So thank you Walt. I count my lucky stars everyday, for the life I have because of you.